(*Continued from back cover*)

She is the quiet partner in the firm, prefers to remain in e background. Many of her clients have never seen her— ow her only as *Dorie,* who suggested a step towards imoved labor relations for a large corporation in a small mmunity; improved relations of personnel with the public a railroad, a hotel, a giant retail chain operation; new licies for special aims for a government department; a plan defeat Communist propaganda aimed at an American corration; a long time approach to problems of geriatrics. hind the scenes, and rarely in the limelight, she has ad-sed many of America's outstanding organizations, publitions, radio broadcasting companies, social welfare comttees and foundations, educational bodies and industrial mpanies. (*"As Eddie's partner I found that he and many our clients treated me as an equal partner, but that the st preferred to believe that woman's place was in the me."*)

She refuses to classify herself as a career woman. (*"Milns of married women work outside the home, and work at me too. There is nothing strange about that."*) While she professional in her office, she claims that she, and most omen of the world, are amateurs in what is generally felt be their main job as homemaker.

Nevertheless she has managed to keep her husband conated with her twenty-four hours a day. She has helped him ar two daughters, both happily married. She has enterned vastly during her life, counting among her friends stinguished men and women from all ranks of life, and om most countries.

Doris Fleischman Bernays is a native New Yorker whose nily was established in that city, and in Albany, New York, er a hundred years ago. She was schooled in the Training epartment of Normal College, now Hunter College, at orace Mann High School, and was graduated from Barnard ollege. She has written almost constantly since she learned form her letters. She has contributed to several books, ited "An Outline of Careers for Women," and has been blished in many magazines on a variety of subjects. nong a great variety of interests and activities, profesnal, eleemosynary and personal, she finds people themves most beguiling and engrossing. Nevertheless she ints that she is an "average woman" whose housewifely oblems are common to all average women.

She has written this book to spotlight the hidden thoughts women at work.

A Wife Is Many Women

A WIFE

Is Many Women

BY DORIS FLEISCHMAN BERNAYS

Crown Publishers, Inc. New York

Library of Congress Catalog Card Number: 55-10170
Printed in the United States of America

TO EDDIE
AND TO DORIE AND DICK
AND TO ANNIE AND JUSTIN

My special thanks go to Justin Kaplan for his helpful suggestions and criticisms. I should like also to thank Howard Cutler and Belle Becker for their careful reading of this manuscript; Stella Kraus and Ann Anderson for their firm grip on details.

CONTENTS

A Wife Is Many Women

CHAPTER ONE

The Magic Aye

My life has been notably quiet and without content, and it can be covered by a few dates.

Sigmund Freud
From a letter to Edward L. Bernays
October 8, 1929

Mr. McGargle, clerk of the Marriage Bureau, was an honest man, but he withheld vital information when he pronounced Eddie and me man and wife in New York's Municipal Building in 1922. He neglected to say that I was thereby licensed and expected to be executive amateur in some twenty-one specialties about which I knew nothing at all.

Men are commonly thought to be frightened at the responsibility of marriage. But like most traditional ideas about the two sexes, this belief is somewhat misleading. It is the bride who ought to faint at the altar. She is about to assume domestic omnipotence as if it were a superwedding gown. And she is agreeing to split her personality into two parts, although most people believe that her two personalities are the same, that woman is synonymous with housewife.

Woman's most remote ancestor undoubtedly had her major occupation in life selected for her when her mate, bored with watching her chew the baby's luncheon, turned his thoughts to the joys of hunting. Picking up a jagged stone, he shuffled out of his murky home, grunting a command over his shoulder, "You stay here. I may be detained late in the forest." His wife meekly gathered leaves and twigs for their couch, kicked them neatly about and pounded the dinner.

This, I am sure, was the start of the world's most successful propaganda campaign—convincing women that hunting (or selling cogwheels) is hard, noble and virile. And, conversely, that housekeeping is easy, womanly and, above all, unworthy of male attention. And *because* she has stayed at home through the ages, woman is equated with a broom. By proof of superior force men have persuaded women that they are equipped by sex to do all the things men don't like to do.

Is woman's place the home? Is the child-bearer also biologically the housekeeper? Are men less domestic than women? Do they resent the confinement of monogamous living? I doubt it. I believe that men are chained as happily to the home as women are. Perhaps even more so, because they have all the fun of individual comfort without the tyranny of domestic minutiae.

Is woman congenitally a better parent than the father could be? All through history this question has been answered in favor of women, although Margaret Mead points to a primitive tribe that traditionally leaves mothering to the fathers. I should like to have some scientific measurement of the latent strength of paternal love. There are so many ideas that assume to be true. There are so many questions that are still unasked.

I am convinced that love and tenderness for children are human traits, not exclusively male or female. Men have inhibited their affection by allowing women to rear children. Women, perhaps needing to prove their superiority in some phase of their lives, have said in effect to men, "You know nothing at all about children. You can't nurse them, can't understand them, can't teach them how to walk. We'll take care of your babies."

Men have always had to leave home, women have had to stay at home, and men have continued to believe that their parental pleasures, duties and abilities were limited by nature. Today, however, men in the United States have more leisure than their fathers ever dreamed of, and women, working outside the home too, devote less time to children. Here is the beginning of a new social culture; the father can demonstrate his talent for fatherhood, the mother can experience the advantages and joys of shared responsibility, and the children can expand in the wholesome atmosphere of a two-parent environment. The new generation, possibly, may mend the chipped walls of the family structure and strengthen family cohesion.

It is statistically and psychologically confusing to classify so much of the world's work under the heading of "Love, wifely and maternal." Only two functions are innately feminine—being a wife and being a mother; both are immeasurably good. Other activities are female *by custom*. Sweeping, sewing, marketing, driving a car or playing a typewriter are unrelated to gender. But we women cannot perform all our tasks with equal competence. Therefore, when we accept care of home and family as our function, we are subject to an enormous amount of criticism.

We seem to be today's scapegoats. Women have taken an awful beating in the past few decades from such partisans as Marynia Farnham, Philip Wylie, and numberless psychologists, sociologists and laymen who blame us for the shortcomings and evils of the adult world. They accuse us of everything from over-protection to child rejection. "You are responsible," they say, "for the aggressors, the timorous, the haters, the immature. You handled them badly in their childhood. You coddled them—or dominated—or neglected them."

Apparently nobody knows precisely what women are. Psychologists and anthropologists have made a start in examining the complex mechanism of the female. But it is not easy to break down the word "sex" into its component parts of biology, function and personality. Miles-Terman tests of male-female attitudes are really no better than polls, because they show only existing attitudes, not what the attitudes might be if culture patterns were different. Anthropologists and social psychologists solemnly wrap up divergent ideas about women in one neat package—and then throw women out of the window.

Perhaps it is no defense to point out that most of us know very little about being a woman when we enter marriage. As far as my own experience went, I was the world's first woman to fall in love, the first wife, the first mother, the first housekeeper, the first newspaper woman to report a prizefight, the first woman partner of a public relations counsel, the first tourist in Guatemala. I learned little from other people's experience, and I do not expect even my daughters to profit by my own. Like most women I have gone into every new experience in a forest-for-the-trees fashion, rarely learning in advance requirements, possibilities, or exactly what my own functions were to be.

A man specializes. He makes money, runs a city, builds bridges, and nothing must interfere with his pursuit. Women have scores of specialties. We turn a screw, pleat a slip cover, diagnose a tantrum, pour a dose, shove a vacuum-cleaner, give a tithe, study a blueprint, fix a leak and exhume our algebra to help our children with their homework. The multiplicity of our tasks has not decreased. In 1750 we had to mold candles; today we must locate a blown fuse. Instead of curing meat, we deep-freeze it.

"Damn it," says Eddie. "I opened the can all over my new English suit. Can you get the spots out?" Although I have no degree in dry cleaning, I sponge and blot while Eddie looks on admiringly. Next morning he examines his good-as-new coat and says, "You're wonderful."

Polygamy has a few advantages. Duties are spread among the wives, instead of being assigned to one woman. In our Western one-wife system of polygamy, each wife is a score of women—housekeeper, mother, plumber, cook, playmate, kept woman and civic asset.

If I wanted schooling for all my jobs—and if there were courses available—it would take a few lifetimes for lessons in cooking, sewing, assorted mechanics, interior decoration, psychology, child care, nursing, medicine, economics, labor relations, social sciences, love, marriage and sex.

Should wives learn to become professional housekeepers? Can they be taught the elements of their complex profession? Only, I believe, if men will consent to learn, too. The effort must be coeducational. Professionalism is not incompatible with love. Yet amateurism is incompatible with intelligence. Do we want to be amateurs who perpetuate the ancient fallacy of a favored class? Woman's status as an amateur is a psycho-emotional survival that is as useful to her as a full-swinging tail would be, had it, too, resisted the processes of evolution. Nevertheless, we are supposed to have mastered dozens of etceterologies without professional training, and to be able to practice them as an amateur (*amo, amas, amateur*).

By definition we are amateurs. The very word is based on the Latin *amare*—to love. We have been amateurs immemorially for love, but for love of a man and of children, not necessarily because we like sweeping. In general we are not housewives for the sake of pecuniary gain, which would rank us as professionals. We are not paid specifically for our work even though our husband traditionally supports us. We are amateurs in the more important sense that we are amateurish. We have little training or specific education in our chosen field. We do not have the professional approach, of wanting to master our work, as doctors, lawyers or architects do. As a corollary, we ourselves and the general population have little respect for this most important of all occupations. In fact, according to the *Encyclopaedia Brittanica,* "the term 'amateur' has acquired a secondary meaning, usually employed somewhat contemptuously, signifying inefficiency, unskillfulness, superficial knowledge or training."

The price men pay for our amateurishness is high. So much time, effort, thought and money are poured into the juggernaut, their home. Our houses too frequently are our masters, ruthless and completely possessive. Little time is left for the delights of life, physical, intellectual, cultural and spiritual. But men continue to cling to the ancient myths and methods of housekeeping. They defeat themselves in rising above the cares of the home. It is their home, too. They might as well make it function as smoothly and as economically as modern science and technology can make it.

If statisticians were to work out a basic wage-hour scale for housewives, men might find to their dismay that their homes cost them more than they earn. At present housework is a concealed expense because our whole economic system is based on free wife-work. Family budgets and balance sheets do not, as a rule, carry her contribution to the home and family care as a labor item, as they do in the case of hired housekeepers. Nor is the wage the wife might earn at outside work considered a loss item.

Let us consider the millions of women who necessarily live on two levels, an amateur level and a wage-earning level.

A good deal of rubbish has been talked about women and careers. Only the word "career" and her vastly increased earning power are new. When my grandmother worked as Grandpa's Saturday night cashier in his New York Fancy Dry Goods Store in 1865, she had no idea she was practicing sex treachery or endangering her marital relationship. And no one suggested she was neglecting her six young children. She merely hopped from need to need. As women did in the Middle Ages, when they were admitted to seventy-two out of eighty-five guilds in England as bakers, tailors, tilers, carpenters and as members of other trades and crafts. My problems of dovetailing duties are the same as those of every double-duty woman no matter what her work is—selling ribbon, driving a taxi or planning a political campaign. Yet we still fool around with the question: "Should women have a home or career?" Circumstances answered the question long ago.

The fact that one married woman out of three or four earns money outside the home in the U. S. has not changed our ideas about the job we are born to, in our sex-caste system. For many of us, outside work is a pleasant escape from the overwhelming muddle of running a home. I find my work as public relations counsel quiet and easy in comparison. Only in my office have I been a professional—trained for the job. In all my other lives—a beginner, a bewildered dolt who has bluffed and tried hard to do an average job as wife, mother and housekeeper.

When I was a girl, marriage was the only self-respecting vocation. To fill in the sterile space between diploma and marriage license one could teach school, do volunteer social work, become a trained nurse, a stenographer, suitably adorned with paper cuffs, or a salesgirl with minute pay and long hours. I have watched the progress of what we used to call the emancipation of women, and freedom to choose one's occupation, until today my friends are a cabinet member, an ambassador, president of a department store, a surgeon, authors, professors of anthropology, architects, publishers, editors, textile designers, sculptors, painters, a dean of a major college and even head of a lighterage company. Whatever their field, however, they have led two lives. Inevitably their work has been halted, as mine has been, to plan a menu for a dinner party arranged for a gregarious husband.

Watching both levels, amateur and wage-earning, has given me the bewildering sensation of living today and living two thousand years ago. As I tackle each new job at home, perplexed and naive, I wonder at the tolerance of men. If industry were as old-fashioned as homes, we should still be riding donkeys instead of airplanes.

Women should not be expected to be expert in all of the fields of housewifery, but they should be able to count on professionals for advice or service. It is the failure of these commercial and professional adjuncts to the job of housewife that make her job so frustrating. When I find myself unable to cope with a stove-repair man who cannot make a top burner level enough for pan-broiling, I look with renewed admiration on men for passing this job on to women.

If men were to apply to the home their scientific training, their research skills, and their systematizing abilities in the handling of routine jobs, they would improve material functions and, consequently, free time and energy to enhance the spiritual values of the home.

If society were to relieve us of some of the petty responsibilities, possibly we might function more effectively in the essentials. Which of our jobs is important enough to focus on? If we decide it is motherhood, as I think we must, give us more time and more training so that we can be wiser and more mature mothers.

Through the need of adjusting to each new job, I have learned a little—here and there. I have found that no one knows very much about the important things of life, such as the interplay of personality and the mechanism of affection. We know too little about too many things, and consequently we are nagged by a continuing sense of guilt. Yet we need not feel guilty about our mistakes or shortcomings because we are dusting as well as we can, cooking to the best of our abilities, and singing lullabies as tenderly as our voices permit.

Lack of training is not a local characteristic. The Journal of the American Medical Women's Association in an important international symposium on housewifery, revealed that in Denmark, New Zealand, Norway, Holland, and in many other countries it is recognized that girls marry without domestic education. Feelings of incompetence among housewives were shown to be a cause of psychological difficulties. Housework, it was suggested, should be invested with greater prestige. The effects of long working hours, overwork, fatigue and infrequent vacations were stressed in this international study.

"Why are women so frustrated?" ask many psychologists. Part of the answer lies in our constant striving for perfection as wife, mother and housewife. Because we like to be all things to one man, we have said yes to every new burden. It is the Magic Aye. The persistent defeat of this striving for perfection creates frustration and piles up a sense of guilt. Because we feel guilty we need to punish ourselves by finding more tasks which we cannot handle. Rarely do we have the thrill of knowing we have done our job well. The architect's sense of accomplishment is not for the mother who tries to stop the weeping of an anxiety-ridden child.

Many of our activities only serve to cover our feelings of inadequacy. They are substitutes. The dust rag is often a weapon of aggression against unattainable perfection.

A distinguished editor once told me, "We men have a tremendous sense of guilt, too, about the work our wives have to do. But there doesn't seem to be much we can do about it. We can pick up a broom, but that doesn't seem to make any essential difference, does it?"

"You help bring up your children, don't you?" I asked. He looked sad. "I'm afraid not. I haven't enough time. And when I get home in the evening I'm very tired."

"Is your wife tired when you get home at night?"

"More tired."

We can't blame men, any more than we can blame women, for the great confusion about responsibilities, delights and privileges.

If there is a villain in this story it is education, which has not decided whether women should be educated as women, whether women who work outside the home are extra-normal and whether men can safely be inducted into the mysteries of family life. We treat students as if they were detached units floating freely in an impersonal society, though we remember that somewhere along the line men should learn something about hygiene, that women should attend a few lectures on sex and marriage, and, if they desire, study home economics. All of us should be taught something about the mechanics of houses, the physical and psychological care of children, and the essential facts of spiritual, emotional and psychological give-and-take in marriage. Education has failed to teach us how to see broad implications in current life, and it has failed to teach us the importance of tapping the reservoir of knowledge in behalf of domestic happiness.

Unfortunately, too many high-school and college girls are again adjusting themselves to the idea that a professional career is an interim job between school and the altar. Today's young women do not know how difficult it was to win the right to choose one's occupation. My generation is alarmed at the tendency of girls to slip back into the kitchen and accept marriage as the outer limit for their creative activity.

The new generation of young married women is brave, but they know little about homemaking. With a cookbook in one hand and a gold band on the other, they attack the great task of keeping the American home intact. Girls who have never baked a cake set out uncomplainingly to cook and mop and, eventually, wheel the baby through the park. "How do you make a fluffy omelet?" asked my teen-aged daughter, Anne. She beamed after I had explained, and said, "Now I can make some man a good wife."

Do I wish that I had drawn on the accumulated wisdom of the world to help me in my most important role as housewife? Undoubtedly, but I know I shall continue to pioneer.

There is so much I should have known about babies, and adolescents, and adults, about my husband. But there was so much living to do, so much loving and yearning, and listening to music and reading and arranging things and hovering, undecided, over expendable details.

Have I done my best? Of course not. I have enjoyed too many things. My own life is typical of all of us who do as well as we know how, and buy a new hat occasionally to divert our minds from the jibes of our conscience. We try to outlive our mistakes.

Although this book is written as if all the jobs of an average housewife are quite different and require different skills and emotions, it seems to me that the total personality is involved in all phases of life. I am I when I bake a cake, when I edit an article, when I pet a cat, nurse a child's cold, try to get my husband to go away on a vacation, try on a dress, coax the butcher to find a small broiler, or arrange a bowl of flowers. Whatever I do, think, feel or believe affects and enhances or detracts from anything else I do. The I-ness of anyone cannot be divided into chapters. Chapters will tell only what the I does, and how the I does it, and how the I likes what it does.

In these pages of hindsight I am not complaining. Nor am I writing an accusation, an exoneration or an apology for all the jobs I have done so badly. Rather, I hope that people will examine the daily lives of women, so full of decisive moments, as well as trivia, which we must handle with the clumsy tools of our inherited cultures. I hope that philosophers, scientists and technologists will study the whole important field of homemaking in the light of modern knowledge, lift it from its amateur pedestal and place it on a firm, true base.

CHAPTER TWO

Lady in the Balcony is Just a Housewife

"Ah, Ischomachus," said I, "that is just what I want to hear from you. Did you yourself train your wife to be of the right sort, or did she know her household duties when you received her from her parents?"

"Why, what knowledge could she have had, Socrates, when I took her for my wife?"

Xenophon, *Oeconomicus*

Can you imagine Secretary Dulles not knowing the difference between a protocol and a White Paper?

That is the kind of housekeeper I am, except that a statesman has a corps of experts to advise and assist him. I was taught nothing about housekeeping or marriage. I knew only that they were insolubly joined in a mystic bond. I had no doubt at all that I could manage to keep my house clean, in repair and furnished properly and serve food to family and friends. All other women could do it, why not I?

Have you ever heard a radio master of ceremonies ask, "You, lady in the balcony, what do *you* do?" You may cringe at her apologetic answer, as I do, "I'm just a housewife." You know there is nothing trivial in being a housewife.

Modern technology and mass production have taken many hard tasks from our soft white hands, such as preparing fresh-plucked feathers for bedding, keeping the smell of cabbage out of milk, and setting a sundial; but basically our houses are not very different from the domestic workshops of our great-grandmothers. We still fight dust, polish silver, pound stuck windows, serve smaller but essentially the same three meals a day, make do with eccentric or inadequate materials, and generally cope with physical crises.

Housekeeping lore today is still a fusty compendium of ancient myths, taboos, awkward methods and muddled philosophy. Man-built homes and woman's work have been at odds ever since primitive functionalism was replaced by urban architectural sophistication. The fragility of the home may be due in part to men's indifference to its structure and function. This means bricks, concrete, steel or even canvas. It means also people. Half a century ago there was a certain rootedness. Today all society is migrating on wheels and wings from community to community. We are forced to trudge from place to place by wars, treaties, famines, tyrannies and seasonal and technical employments.

To counteract this change from a static to a migrant era and to keep together the remnants of our family institution, we have only the devotion of men and women to home as an idea. Where this devotion breaks down the family is shattered. The basic knowledge of what a home means somehow got lost on the road to town.

Today's houses have not caught up with modern sciences and skills. Yesterday's houses were designed, undoubtedly, by idiots, maniacs, or woman-haters. The maximum of elegance within the social-economic frame took precedence in architects' plans. The minimum of working convenience was what the home got.

I thought houses were efficient working units until I had to run them. Although I saw to it that they were always pleasant places to live in, they were dragons that devoured workers.

Whether it has one hand, self-employed, or many hands under management, a home is a factory, and the house and the labor to run it should be considered together. Women have managed the personnel problem so unimaginatively that they have driven the majority of professional domestic workers from the field.

My childhood home on East 48th Street, a model of simple unfunctionalism, was a charming brownstone house of three stories and basement, with a high stoop entrance for company, and an under-the-stoop entrance for everybody else. The basement was in constant use. Its front dining room, cozy and sunny, was our study and game room. Because the kitchen was in the rear, looking out on the yard, the cook had to walk down the long hall to answer the front doorbell and to conduct her business with the outside world.

The second floor was well-used. Moth and Pop slept in the folding bed in the family sitting room, and my sister, my baby brother and I slept in our parents' bedroom in back, with its massive uxorious mahogany furniture and a crib. As we got measles and grew older, there was a constant shifting about to find appropriate sleeping and sitting-room space and privacy for two adults and four children in three rooms.

The parlor floor was hardly ever used. In the back there was a company dining room filled frequently with ladies dressed in pale blue or tan broadcloth dresses decorated with many little buttons, long sweeping trains and large puffy sleeves. They gushed approval of us as they sipped chocolate, their little fingers daintily extended. At a few formal dinner parties, vaguely remembered, the rumbling dumbwaiter provided large platters for the lace-covered candle-lit table.

The front parlor, antedating Gertrude Stein's *Four Saints in Three Acts* by half a century, had plump angels floating in thick white clouds on a blue ceiling that gave me an abiding love of fairy tales, magic and virtue. They were related esthetically to the tan walls and mahogany trim, hand-painted to imitate wood graining.

In the upstairs dining room, lights turned low, my brother Leon read Poe to Bea and me and gave me an unconquered fear of the dark. Otherwise the parlor floor was kept safe from the activities that crowded the rooms above and below.

The high stoop, however useless as an entrance to our everyday life, served as backstop for bouncing balls, as steps to play jacks on, and as a romantic porch on balmy evenings, provided you had straw mats. No one used the fine iron balcony in front of the high parlor windows.

We had a lovely, spacious back yard, useful for burying canaries, playing house and planting pansies among the peonies, roses, syringa and Rose of Sharon which, in my memory, seem to have bloomed constantly and simultaneously.

Grandpa and Grandma lived next door, their house and back yard almost like ours, and an open door in the dividing white wooden fence. On the other side lived my cousin Denise, but there was no door between our yards, so we loosened a board in the fence and crawled through to visit. In that back yard we swore to be good, signed our names in blood on a piece of paper and buried it. Denise was an only child, worried over by a meticulously pompadoured mother and a smiling father who always sat on a doughnut cushion because there was something wrong with him.

Our family had two maids, generally considered the correct number to care for a three-story-and-basement house and provide some leisure for the housekeeper. The downstairs girl cooked and cleaned, and the upstairs girl was chambermaid, nursemaid, laundress and waitress. Moth worked at marketing and a number of other unperceived things during the day, and did the mending at night while Pop read history.

Moth was not considered part of the labor force. She was, however, a vigorous housekeeper. "I had to be," she explained. "A large house, four children bringing in friends all the time, and only two in help." Up and down a ladder she climbed slowly and with dignity, plucking crystals from the chandelier, dipping them in a pan, and reaching them back onto the wire hooks where they trembled and glittered.

I watched and felt a strange love, either for her or the activity. It was noble, but it was not expected of me.

She had a job, she adjusted to it cheerfully and was happy in it. Mother's generation worked seriously at home-making. But they must have considered it inferior work, because they encouraged us to avoid it.

When I was sixteen years old I became engaged for a little while and spent a good deal of time day-dreaming about being a housewife standing happily in a pretty pantry. Keeping house was my only vision of married life.

We were brought up in an age when servants, as they used to be called, were an inherent part of the middle-class pattern of life. My own lack of training was based on the assumption that someday I was going to be second-in-command in a home, with hired help to take over most of my duties.

My amateur status as manager was firmly established when Eddie and I crossed the threshold of our first home. It wasn't until three days later, when Eddie and I surveyed a noble mahogany bed Moth had given us, two chairs, a card-table, spoons, forks and knives for two, and a few cooking utensils—all the equipment in our lovely converted stable in Washington Mews—that I realized I was a housewife. *I* was responsible for clean sheets on the bed and for the food promised by the spoons. I wondered vaguely what to do next, but assumed that everything would work out as automatically as it had at home when I was a girl the week before. It was not destined to be quite so automatic.

I left the house early next morning with Eddie. Between writing an outline for a public relations campaign for the New York City Hotel Association and the Welcome, Stranger Committee that Eddie had organized to encourage visitors to come to the city, and writing a story about the Beaux Arts Ball, I telephoned an agency for a maid, interviewed cooks without having the faintest notion what questions to ask, and returned home with Eddie at seven o'clock.

This, our first home, was a cinch for a totally inexperienced housekeeper. Choy, our houseman, became acting head, with full power and responsibility. When Choy returned to Korea to practice medicine, Kim took over. My management role, after engaging an able executive, was to count noses of guests, turn bills over to our bookkeeper at the office and buy necessary pots, soap and curtains. This, however, was my last opportunity to play house.

We moved into 8 Washington Square North one month before our first child was born. We moved in gaily, too ignorant about housekeeping matters to wonder why there were eleven servants' rooms on the top floor. We learned before long that this beautiful example of Federal architecture had been designed for the destruction of the servant class, caste, or profession. Household help was expected to race up and down long graceful stairways answering batteries of bells. Our houseman saved steps by carrying two heavy trays on his palms up and down two flights three times a day to the nursery.

A visiting friend, an engineer, laughed when I told him the doctor had said I seemed overworked. He pulled out an envelope and pencil and figured that I climbed the Eiffel Tower every day. "Too much for any woman," he said, shaking his head.

I guessed that the help climbed Mt. Everest each day, and we abandoned the house very soon afterward.

Architects built so many difficulties into such houses that only a great expenditure of physical labor could keep the plant running. This was especially so in the houses Eddie rented all over the Jersey Coast, Westchester and nearby Connecticut to give our children fresh air and motorless play during the summers. Our various landlords were delighted to share their burden for a few months during the depression.

I felt guilty about living in these pretentious monsters. They embarrassed me. They represented an ostentatious attitude toward wealth and expenditure that had no relationship to my life. Furthermore, they contained every pompous device that architects could devise to harass housekeepers, even in the prosperous eras in which they had been erected.

One house had four pantries on the main floor; one pantry for a breakfast room, for a dining room, for flowers, and a fourth, possibly, for in-between snacks. Another house had a large closet with twelve shelves for twelve complete breakfast sets and trays to feed pampered guests in comfort.

In an Italian *palazzo* set in a lush Westchester forest a huge old coal stove dominated a ballroom-sized kitchen. To keep this stove burning, someone had to go down a steep flight of stairs to the cellar, walk to a coal pile nearly a hundred feet away, back again with filled coal scuttle and up the stairs to poke the stove and empty the ashes. I rented a canned-gas stove, but the coal stove won out. The kitchen maid came to me to give notice: "Cook makes me get up at four every morning to get the coal stove burning for breakfast. Even Sunday."

Whatever their style of architecture, Oklahoma-Gothic, Westchester-Tudor, or Chinese-General Grant, they all looked like Westminster Abbeys to me—stupendous, archaic and impossible to run efficiently, if I had cared to try.

When large houses fell into private disuse, architects of small homes, with less room for error, failed to solve the problem of building for function. In a northern New Jersey real estate development my sister and I looked one day at ranch and split-level houses ranging in price from $17,000 to $37,000. We asked the polite agent who showed us through one of these compact dwellings, "Where does the lady keep her brooms and vacuum cleaner and pail? And where is the storeroom for trunks and suitcases?"

He looked bewildered at first. "Mop and pail closet?" His face cleared. "In the garage, I guess." We looked. No room in the garage for even a flat broom. I have not yet figured out how the owner solved her problem. There was not an inch for a utility closet in the entire house.

To simplify our way of life we tried living at the Sherry-Netherland Hotel, where keeping house was even more difficult because we tried to serve home-cooked meals on a tiny portable electric stove. Then a luxury apartment on Fifth Avenue, which we vacated very quickly because the landlord was stingy about heat and refrigeration, and finally, in 1940, to 163 East 63rd Street.

"Don't buy a house," the late Lucius Boomer, president of the Waldorf Astoria, warned Eddie. "You will never be able to find a staff to do the work." We stubbornly moved in and have had little trouble in spite of wars, labor shortages and minor construction difficulties. The front and back doors are some fifty feet apart as the cook flies, and when both bells ring at the same time, there is widespread panic. Possibly we get along in a short labor market because the house is cheery, and because we have been indifferent to details.

It seemed occasionally that one was less a mother, wife and public relations counsel than an employment agency and personnel manager for all these winter and summer houses. Engaging new help for changed conditions was a gamble based on hunches. References were often unreliable. "She's a good plain cook," might mean, "I never want to taste her stewed steaks again." If you liked their blue eyes, their taste in hats, you took a chance, using extra-sensory perception. Whatever the mechanics of choice, our statistical average of success has been very high.

After living in a dozen country and city houses I developed a few rules for running a house without knowledge or training.

Rule I. Be an executive. An executive takes for granted that others can do what he can't do himself.

Rule II. Most things had better be ignored. Today I feel

that a torn chair is a mark of valor. I couldn't have survived otherwise.

Rule III. People assume responsibility when you refuse to take over. Things run much more efficiently and happily without amateur interference.

Rule IV. Always be pleasant.

Rule V. Bluff whenever you are in doubt about methods or protocol.

At first I didn't know enough to try to assign duties to employees but talked vaguely about specific jobs, hoping they knew what they were supposed to do. It was sheer luck that they did.

During years of comfortable aloofness I devised an executive system. Each new employee was given a detailed schedule in fifteen-minute periods of daily activities, allowing for interruptions. Hall closets 11:15 to 12 on Tuesdays. Workers accepted these schedules enthusiastically, looked at them admiringly for a minute and then put them away forever.

Occasionally I have wondered how other women learned to be such excellent housekeepers. Who taught them and when? Tradition, in a changing technological world?

Perhaps I might have learned if I had listened to domestic conversations, but I found little to amuse me in domestic shop talk that circled drearily around misdeeds of workers. The tone was generally an angry whine. After a few minutes of this my ears would try to pick up a bit of masculine conversation.

I asked Madame Pandit what women in diplomatic circles talk about. "In Washington?" she asked. "Yes." "They talk about clothes and servants," she said somewhat bitterly. "What do they talk about in India?" I asked. "In diplomatic circles?" "Yes." She smiled. "Clothes and servants."

One evening we visited a woman who takes pride in her housekeeping. Every chair, every plate, every lamp, every flower filled its allotted place as if they were precision-tooled.

Now here, I thought, is a woman, tight-lipped though she may be, who can tell me what a housewife does all day. I still don't know because she left me after a minute to empty an ash-tray, peer into an ice bucket and shove a chair.

A group of women at Erich Leinsdorf's house in Larchmont one evening agreed that they were hit-and-miss housekeepers, too. One woman said she had never made a bed. Another confessed that she went to a hotel when her maid left.

"It's the same all over the world," said a middle-aged Frenchwoman. "Nowhere are women properly taught how to keep house."

"Too bad there aren't more schools all over the country like our housekeeping academy," said a Cincinnati woman.

A few weeks later I visited her pleasant broom-and-brush college in Cincinnati. Following the sound of dull drumbeats, I was led to a large front parlor, where I saw a sweet-faced woman waving her arms as a tall, sober man thumped a velvet cushion in time to her downbeat. In other classrooms I saw men and women polish floors, iron sheets and stir pots. On my way out, three-quarters of an hour later, the woman was still showing the large man how to plump a pillow.

Hunter College and City College in New York have given instruction in almost everything a housekeeper ought to know: very short courses in child psychology, learning French with your children, family problems, how to make lampshades, draperies or slipcovers, minor household repairs, elementary woodwork, decoration, clothing design, textiles, millinery and financial planning.

Unfortunately my children showed no desire at any time, while in our home, to do or learn anything about the craft of homemaking, which has now become a minor major in their own homes. There, I gather, they cheerfully, and with some effectiveness, carry on their household work after office hours, performing largely in traditional ways.

When they lived with us they learned little about the pervasive, obvious or invisible functions of housekeeping. I taught them nothing. On the contrary, I enjoyed coming home to find our entrance hall piled high with shoulder bags, books, gloves, scarves and even shoes. The children are home, I thought. A maid tried in vain to make them keep their own rooms neat, a job finally accomplished by camp and college.

My young daughter Anne told me that she was so terrified when she started housekeeping last summer that she wouldn't go to the supermarket alone. Her husband, protesting but probably flattered, went along as supporting cast.

But today's young women are courageous and eager and they learn with enormous speed.

My daughter Doris and her husband Dick have solved their problem by living cooperatively with six of their friends. They disregard any inhuman demands of their monster, and bow only to the essential needs of a home. They clean, not for the sake of cleaning, but only for the sake of cleanliness. They cook not to impress, but only to nourish and amuse. They are not obsessed by a need to keep up standards. It has worked happily for several years.

I am always interested in other women's reactions to the job of housekeeping. Many women love it. It is the job to which they have looked forward all their lives, and it is the satisfying answer to their aspirations. They like to work a room into good shape, they love to clean, clean, clean, like Nellie, who combed the fringes of rugs into straight neat lines until someone reminded her that rug fringes, unlike hair, don't grow. Heaven preserve me from compulsively meticulous women, whether they drive themselves or their subordinates mad. Beautiful, soulful Aunt Rose kept house with steady resentment for fifty years. I believe she wanted to paint. I saw some pictures she had done "when I was a girl," and asked her why she didn't take up her art again.

"Pooh," she answered. "I have no time for such things." Our great frustration is the inescapable need to do one job while we would prefer to do another. The sex-caste system takes its toll in unhappiness.

My mother, on the other hand, had a certain elegant carelessness about details. In other homes children must not spot rugs or sit on the best chairs. The sanctity of our home did not extend to furniture. Eddie and I have carried on the tradition that people are more important than the house or its mechanics. When we were married we swore that if any *thing* became important to us we would toss it out of the window.

However, even after years of training myself to be above material preoccupations, my enjoyment of our own parties is still dimmed by the mechanics of hospitality. Matches, chairs, draughts, heat, gravy before the meat grows cold lure my attention from the most fascinating conversation.

Professor James Feibleman says, from the depths of an easy chair, "Philosophy should employ the scientific method. We must search for universals in human nature." "Wonderful," I answer, "but what universals?" Instead of listening while he tells me what I yearn to know, my ears desert him and tune in on the stairs, waiting for the sound of Albert's announcing feet. What is delaying dinner?

Open dissatisfaction with housework keeps pace with the need to engage in it. Young married women tell me of their weariness, of how they are "tied down," a phrase that I detest. A twenty-three-year-old mother of three said, "I love my home. But after three hours of clearing up other people's papers, books, shoes and gloves, I wonder if my love is a normal one."

"Nonsense," said another young mother in long, slim trousers, "women love housekeeping. I love to cook and sew and make things neat and shiny."

"If you had good help to do it for you, would you like that?" I asked.

"Of course, any woman would."

What compulsion drives us? Do we want to prove we are martyrs? Are we afraid we shall be unfeminine if we look for more efficient ways? We adhere to ancient attitudes unconsciously absorbed and without understanding why. We still try to keep men on pedestals, serene and safe from dishtowels, butchers' hand-weighted scales and hurried resettings of tables to seat unexpected guests.

The house must run so smoothly that no one, especially the husband, can see the effort. For instance, just as you leave the office late one afternoon, Eddie says casually, "I invited those five men for dinner tonight."

"Excuse me a minute, I've forgotten my gloves," you say, go back to your desk and telephone home.

The day we moved into our new house at 163 East 63rd Street with no maid at all, Eddie arrived home unexpectedly a day early with the two children whom he had called for at camp and two of their friends. A frantic surreptitious hunt for sheets, cots and paper plates saved Eddie the pain of being disillusioned about me.

Human relations are the housewife's greatest and most constant problem. She is umpire. She is pacifier. She must be sensitive to people's moods, but must never have moods herself. She must be soothing syrup, ego-booster, but never cross.

Doctors used to ascribe female neuroses to idleness. In the development of modern psychosomatics, women are neurotic because they overwork, and they overwork because they are neurotic.

How can you figure energy output in running a home? You would have to multiply square yards by baby's hunger, times papa's lost fishing rod, plus the cube of John's cornet and divide by inertia. Someone who knows how to measure such things reckoned that a young mother today puts in about 100 hours of work per week. It is true that a washing machine, a mangle and other mechanical aids may cut a few minutes from this total. Diaper service will make a further cut in time, provided the young husband can pay for it. But anyone of my generation who does a little baby-sitting will admit this estimate is valid.

On the whole, today's young mothers work almost as long and as hard as our pioneer ancestors, who knew nothing about frozen foods or taxiing their families around the countryside. One of the great differences is that our ancestors had plenty of volunteer helping hands. There were grandmothers, maiden aunts and daughters to share the endless tasks. Today, grandmothers no longer live with their children. Maiden aunts have their own careers, daughters go to college and become department-store executives, secretaries and airplane hostesses.

I am exceedingly lazy and therefore cannot claim that I am an overworked housekeeper. I felt overworked only in the summers when we had so many guests that someone talked me to sleep every night, and someone sitting on my bed talked me awake in the morning. Faces, names and personalities stopped having any meaning for me.

"How do you find time to work at your office, take care of your children and your home and entertain so much?" people ask me frequently. It is a simple problem in temporal mathematics. The relativity of time and motion is wholly practical. "Everything falls into a twenty-four-hour schedule if you ignore non-essentials, such as cocktail parties, and focus on what you care most about, like playing with your children," Mrs. Millicent McIntosh said when she was Headmistress of the Brearley School and had five children.

The great trick is to weed out unnecessary activities, and then to divide essentials into two categories. The first group can be characterized as expendable necessities. The second group or residue can be defined as reducible necessities. These can be shrunken by the application of systems, short-cuts and other technical devices.

For instance, to facilitate moving, I worked out an elaborate system of labeling, tagging, numbering, room mapping, and letting the movers do all the packing and unpacking. But my systems were never quite adequate, as could be testified by kind and understanding insurance companies who replaced lost barrels of pots and pans, blankets, silver, linens, mirrors and *prie-dieux*. Surely there must be a foolproof way of transplanting one's possessions. Until I find it I shall never move again.

I think I won't, but undoubtedly the day will come when we shall become bored with our home. The street will seem too noisy, the sun too hot, the rain too pervasive, the kitchen too large, the doors too far away, the yard too sooty. In short, we shall want the new personality of a new home.

It has always amused me to watch how people seem to vary in different settings. They put on the characteristics of a place as if it were a psychic costume. A woman is not the same person in an art gallery as she is in the supermarket. Our friends have changed their personalities to match our walls. In Washington Mews they were carefree, intimate and Left Bank. In Washington Square they were stately and impressive until Prohibition applejack washed out their inhibitions. On Fifth Avenue they became so stuffy and refined that we moved away after three years. On East 63rd Street they seem somehow to be themselves—relaxed, intellectual, dogmatic, esthetic, sometimes bawdy.

Swimming pools make even philosophers boisterous. Poets play discus with five-and-ten-cent dishes, government officials toss one another into the chlorine blue. I shudder to think what delayed effects may show up in our children, who seemed to react so normally to this mixed diet of domiciles.

Wherever it was, they continued to behave as if the place where they lived was home.

No matter where one lives, it is always a challenge to find the right technicians to eliminate the cracks and spots of time. When the door sticks, the locksmith says it's a carpenter's job, but the carpenter says it's a locksmith's job. That can go on for weeks.

Recently I heard about a plumber who used uranium in his work. But my plumber spent $17.50 worth of time to take off a radiator cover, put a new valve on the radiator and glue the radiator-cover splinters together again. Plumbers may be good at atomic house wrecking, but I am convinced that automation is not yet a threat to the housekeeper's job.

I quote here, with permission, an item that still seems good to me, although I clipped it from the December 9, 1950, issue of the *New Yorker*:

"A professional woman who is having a new drainboard built on her kitchen sink came home the other evening to find the following note from the officiating carpenter:

" 'Casing too wide, has to be trimmed. Nothing standard any longer! May be able to finish this week, but will not be in tomorrow. Must take a movie in, otherwise go batty.' "

Oil burners break down at Christmas, air conditioners stop on the Fourth of July, and coal gases from the house next door make one wonder what the lining of our babies' lungs look like.

House temperatures defeat me. Come winter, come summer. Furnaces, radiators, weather and inhabitants, all disagree. Eddie likes a hothouse, I like a breeze, my daughters don't care as long as they can kick off their shoes. I thought that heat rationing during the fuel shortage would simplify matters because the thermostat could be set finally and unchangeably at sixty-five degrees. But our cook's boy friend insisted she needed, or was entitled to, eighty degrees.

Dry cleaning clothes often awakens deep philosophic

thoughts in a housekeeper. Georgia O'Keefe showed clearly how troublesome this problem could be. She came into a small restaurant on Lexington Avenue to join us at lunch with a pair of trousers dangling from her left arm.

"Stieglitz," she said vaguely, holding them up to show her husband, "I have been going up and down the avenue trying to find someone to press your pants, but I can't find a tailor."

It was easy to sympathize with her. My secretary had just spent half a day riding around in a taxi trying to find someone to mend a wobbly card table.

I have for many years tried to find a way to get enough bookshelves built so that books would stop piling up on tables, chests of drawers and even creeping into closets. I think I should like a portable electric typewriter in every room. One well-lit, full-length mirror would be pleasant, too.

I dream now and then, wherever I live, of making what architects call structural changes. I should like to eliminate a vacuum caused by a stairway covering one-third of the house's space. I should love to push down a thick wall without, like Samson, bringing the house down on my head. I should like to turn three queerly placed closets into one sensible space. I'd like to put something up, take something down, move it here, move it there. Anything would improve any house built by an architect of any old school.

A few of my friends discussing their lives as professionals and as housekeepers said that men ought to care more how their money is spent.

A public relations woman said, "That is where the present generation is smarter than we were. Now there are househusbands as well as housewives. They recognize that it's a man's home, too. Husbands change the babies, bathe them and feed them. They cook when their wives are busy, go marketing, and help with the dishes. They don't seem to feel that a dishrag neutralizes virility."

"Well," another woman contradicted, "my husband would think he had lost his manhood if he found the handle of a vacuum cleaner in his fingers."

"Does he think housekeeping is a sex characteristic?"

"Lots of men think that," said a dress designer. "I heard a doctor on a radio program chuckle like mad as he told the audience that he had announced the birth of a daughter to a very nervous father in this way: 'I said to him, a fine little dishwasher is born to you this day.' He thought a dishpan was female."

"The thing that riles me is that housekeeping has no status at all," said a teacher who is famous for her goulash and for her knowledge of medieval literature. "Nobody ever says to the housewife: 'You are an artist.' I have heard them say it to bricklayers and chefs, but do husbands ever say it to their favorite sweeper-upper?"

Housework is drudgery. Housework is as bare of laurels as the last horse in a steeplechase. Women will continue doing it because women are born with brooms in their mouths.

What is the solution?

We need a change in our approach to the whole question of house-building and home-making. Let us treat the subject as if it were a science cluster. Let us endow a study of the abstract philosophic and sociologic concept of home. Let us also endow pure research, laboratory experimentation and fieldwork, perhaps in institutions such as the Massachusetts Institute of Technology. The abstract idea, home, would be divided into its component parts: a machine, a workshop, a convenience, a nursery, and a love-and-pleasure palace.

Almost all the important changes that have been introduced into the home in the past centuries have come through men, usually through men who have wanted to make money by selling objects for other men's homes. If we are to have any profound improvement, let us put men's inventiveness, their genius for organizing and their general know-how to the creation of comfort, convenience and economy in their own homes.

If a few hundred men with vision and daring and management skill took charge of running their homes, we would undoubtedly profit by a much-needed revolution. They would apply their special knowledge to the rewarding task of bringing the home into the twentieth century. They would not long be content with archaic and cumbersome techniques. For example, an airplane has a central control panel, but my house has half a dozen fuse boxes concealed in closets, under staircases and behind cellar doors.

It takes half a day to wash our windows; chemical pipes and ducts could cleanse them automatically. Kitchens might be hosed from top to bottom, the water running out through a floor drain. A one-man mattress turner would be good if we must have mattresses, although research ought to devise a clean simple sleeping arrangement that differs from our present cumbersome bed as an air-conditioner differs from a palm-leaf fan. Why not vermin-proof all equipment and materials, remove dust automatically? Light-interrupters would permit us modestly to keep shades up and let summer breezes in. Our technicians are devilishly smart. They can do anything. They would study the home as a whole engineering unit and apply mass methods to planning, flow of work, cleaning and provisioning.

If the making of a house were elevated to the status of a science, where it properly belongs, our houses would be homes instead of careers and we should have more time for the pleasant intangibles of family and community life.

CHAPTER THREE

Women are Funny about Money

As for money, enough is enough; no man can enjoy more.

Robert Southey, *The Doctor*

I have always thought that $50.00 was a nice sum of money, and two cents was just right. Grandpa gave his grandchildren a $50.00 gold piece on each birthday. Mother had $50.00 a week allowance to pay her household expenses. Two cents was my weekly allowance for many years.

I have had other fixed financial ideas. During my adolescence I thought $3,000.00 was the right sum of money to start marriage on. Later I knew that $20,000.00 was the right price of a house. I even thought that ten per cent was the right amount for a tip to a waiter. Most women I have known are funny about money.

Men, too, of course. Many people thought my father's attitude was eccentric. He despised money and ignored it as much as possible. I never heard him talk about it. As a young lawyer from Albany in his new partnership of Fleischman and May, he had charged staggeringly small fees. I know because I have seen an entry of $2.75 for making out a will in his checkbook of 1896 and a charge of $3.75 for pleading a case in court. He never accepted a client whom he did not consider legally, ethically and morally right.

Although my generous mother felt that she ought not to spend money on herself but on other people, she was intensely practical. She knew how to get a good deal out of a dollar. She knew a bargain when she saw it, and at eighty-eight called my bookkeeper to remind her that dividends were due.

I never heard Moth disagree with Pop about money, but I learned that some wives wept because their husbands were strangely cruel about money. On Moth's At Homes on alternate Thursdays, I heard low-voiced horror tales of women who got tradesmen to pad their bills and return the difference to them. I heard of women who had to pay everything by check and were not allowed any spending money at all. This was true only of the carriage trade with charge accounts. One woman cried into her chinchilla jacket because she said her husband was stingy. A pretty woman sipping chocolate said to Mother in a whining voice, "I don't know what to do any more. I think my husband is having business reverses but he won't tell me anything about it. I don't know whether I should dismiss any of my maids or shop more economically. What should I do?" Mother didn't know either. Women were naturally bashful about discussing money with their husbands. Money talk was as taboo as sex talk.

Bewildered by these social-economic revelations, I put on my coat, patted my war button, "To Hell with Spain, Remember the Maine," and went outdoors to meditate. I watched the cross-patch lamplighter turn the gas key. The little blue and yellow flame jumped from his stick and signaled the darkness to advance. Was it that evening that I asked him, "Who are you going to vote for?" and he answered violently, "Go to Hell"? Eddie says that was my first contact with venality. Something may have gone wrong with the lamplighter's deal in the brisk market for votes.

Fifty years later I heard an echo of financial frustration when I found a young woman wiping her eyes and blowing her nose in our hostess' bedroom.

"I know you'll think I'm silly," she apologized, "but I had to come in for a cry when my husband told everybody in there that he thought all women should have a thorough knowledge of finance."

"What is sad about that?"

"Do you know he took away my checking account two years ago because I overdrew a little? He gives me money every day for taxis and lunch and things like that. I can charge whatever I want. But I have had to learn how to hoard. I splurge and buy things I don't want for spite."

A few years ago a woman told me sadly, "He says we must cut down expenses. Then I wonder what expenses, and how much. A week later he gives me a lavish amount. I can't budget, although I'd love to. I don't know what his income is or anything. I think it's terrible."

"Can't you talk frankly to him?" I asked.

"Did you ever hear of anyone changing the mind of a judge? He makes decisions at home, too. He says, 'Women—you can't let them know anything. They'd dip in and take everything.' "

Until Eddie forced into me some theoretical knowledge and some practical steps in household economics, I was as illiterate economically as any overprotected nineteenth-century woman.

This was not my mother's fault. She was financially astute and careful, because she had learned about money when she was a child in the early 1870's. Before she had reached her teens she had measured yards of goods and computed costs in Grandpa's dry-goods store. She had collected rents from the property he owned on East 5th Street, and acquired an interest in real estate that was still evident when she was in her eighties and reading real estate news in *The New York Times.*

Unfortunately, I was brought up on the principle of allowances and extra handouts. Certainly I was never taught anything about basic values. My two cents allowance grew to five, to ten, to twenty-five, to fifty, and finally to the comforting sum of a dollar and a half when I was a student at Barnard College. I didn't know that there was such a thing as a budget and had not the faintest idea what my annual clothes expenditure was. I didn't know what the tuition fee at college was. I did take a boring, impractical and unenlightening course in economics under blushing young Benjamin Anderson, later economist of the Chase National Bank, but I had no idea what he was talking about. I can remember only his lecture on socialism, possibly because it sounded so unreal. I was born a Republican.

After sixteen years of schooling, I was a complete financial idiot, and went out into the world unprepared to handle anything but nickels and dimes.

Earning my living should have, but didn't, teach me anything about finances. I started to work at $15.00 a week as reporter and feature writer on the New York *Tribune*. As assistant woman's page and assistant Sunday editor, I received $22.00. But Pop continued to pay my way through life. My salary was extra and unimportant. One day I handed a bundle of uncashed checks through the cage of the Clark Bank in the Tribune Building at 154 Nassau Street. An outraged teller leafed through them and called for an officer. The two scowling men came around and confronted me. "Don't you know you've upset the bookkeeping system of the *Tribune* by holding checks for three months?" A few years later, when Eddie asked what salary I wanted in his first small office at 19 East 48th Street, I said firmly, "I can't work for less than $45.00 a week." He looked so surprised I knew I should have asked for more. But I was still letting Pop support me.

The first time I thought about my own finances was when I wondered why I wasn't getting interest on the balance of $100 in my bank book. A penny at compound interest deposited by Nero, I had learned, would be worth billions by then, 1920. I asked the teller in John Marquand's Fifth

Avenue Bank to give me some interest. Gravely he explained, "We do not give interest on checking accounts." I decided to resign from his bank. I was surprised and faintly humiliated that he didn't care.

Poor Eddie. He tried to teach me elementary facts and practices soon after we were married, but I was totally untrained as a purchasing agent. He discovered, for instance, that I put bills anywhere, not even wondering who would pay them. He tried to teach me how to pay them, how to keep my checkbook properly. I used up erasers, and ink eradicators burned holes in the stubs. At one embarrassing session, he saw that I had $10,000 left over from $1,000.

Eddie was patient, and I was a conscientious failure. A $3.60 check came back stamped "no funds." In terror of imprisonment, I drove to the small bank at North Long Branch and confessed my crime. The president himself sat down with me, looked over my stubs, and found I had overdrawn by $12.73. He was so sorry for me that he spent more than an hour calling up the three merchants involved, the clearing house, and for all I could understand, the United States Treasury at Washington to save my reputation. I gave up. Our bookkeeper, Stella Kraus, a wise and patient woman, now takes care of my bills and checks and taxes.

Eddie tried to teach me to spend money, but I couldn't seem to find time.

"It's your money, why don't you buy yourself something nice?"

But if you had been trained in childhood to be thrifty, making certain that you bought sensibly and practically; if you frequented Grey's drugstore, the famous New York bargain basement for theatre tickets; if you had stood at the opera, and subscribed to a dress circle seat at the New York Symphony; if, in other words, you had been indoctrinated with the idea that waste makes want, then it becomes very hard to learn how to buy luxuries, how to join the ranks of the financially carefree and extravagant. After more than thirty years of practice, I have not improved much in this branch of economy. Spending one's own or one's father's or husband's funds depends on one's point of view, usually acquired early. New attitudes can be learned when conditions are favorable to change.

Eddie tried next to teach me a few fundamentals in economics. He explained dividends, shares, stocks, bonds, arbitrage, rates of exchange. I understood perfectly in the abstract, but he overestimated my intelligence when he expected me to clip coupons. Anthropology got the best of me in a bank vault. It had the odor of oil and steel, of relentless sanctity. It was sacred, taboo. I was a guilty, excited invader of its intricate mechanism of bolts, bars and cells, and trembled before the fat tutelary gods in blue uniform. We gave that up, and I was free and happy again.

Years later Eddie and I believed, perhaps because of my ignorance, that we should try to give our children some inkling of cause and effect between money and things they needed or desired. However, we kept putting off the day. It had shocked me to hear of eight-year-old children having to keep account books of their expenditures. It seemed obvious that this would make a civilization of adults who were overly attentive to monetary values.

When Doris and Anne were around seventeen and eighteen years old, it seemed necessary at last to put them on an allowance. Only by paying for their own clothes and entertainment could they learn how to manage their funds later on. Eddie agreed and had, in fact, recommended some sort of instruction for several years.

I had no idea how much money they might need in an inflationary period. This was during the war, when we were accustomed to instability, a little more than a decade after inflation had made us aware of the power of money. How could I foretell how much stockings, school lunches, coats, would go up? I might give them far too much and the lesson in practical management would have negative results. Or, if I gave them too little I might add to the sense of insecurity that was part of their contemporary heritage.

The first time that economics became a dramatic force in my life was in the late twenties. Even people who had thought the subject dull, academic and unreal, opened their imaginations and learned, as I did, that index figures and lines on graphs were worth thinking about.

From 1926 to 1936 we swung through great inflation and depression. In 1939 to 1946 we adjusted and readjusted to the violent needs of war preparation, then recovery, with shortages of consumer production before and after. Now in 1955 we are threatened with a new inflation of possibly serious proportions.

In these periods of upheaval, economics was not a question of our personal earning power, of family budgeting and consumption, or of saving. It was living through cosmic conditions like hurricanes, heat waves, zero snaps and floods. Melodramatic economic weather was our climate. There was no ignoring or minimizing its nationwide or even worldwide power.

The Great Inflation of the twenties had started to change the American scene. It was a financial aphrodisiac: eyes glittered, hands waved, feet danced and voices caroled. Everyone was manic. As pretty price bubbles sailed through the air, people tried to catch them in infantile glee. They became exhibitionists showing their naked pleasure in wealth.

There was only one topic of conversation—the stock market. Elevator men asked for market tips on the way up, and gave you stock tips on the way down. Stock brokers called us up every few minutes suggesting American Tel & Tel, and Air Reduction, and Radio Corporation, and Electric Bond and Share. In our family, Eddie handled all this, while I sat back in disbelief and bewilderment. Only once did I take an active part.

A charming old gentleman during dinner at our home said, "I like you. I am going to give you a tip: tomorrow morning, at the opening of the market, buy Mohawk Carpet Company." Next morning Eddie's broker bought 100 shares. I was frightened and the next day sold them. The profit of $3,000 made me feel like a kept woman.

I have resisted, all my life, taking money seriously except as an indispensable aid in sickness and senescence. Eddie, on the other hand, has always gone very deeply into any subject that interested him. While he was enjoying the rising market, he was also making a profound study of economics. He soon decided that brokers had only superficial knowledge. Our living room on Washington Square was a battleground for the conflicting ideas of economists who gathered around Eddie because they wanted his specialized knowledge of public psychology. They, too, were exhilarated and disturbed by rising index figures and market quotations regularly preceded by plus signs. How would the public react, how could emotions be harnessed or channeled?

Carl Snyder, statistician of the Federal Reserve Bank of New York, our close friend, brought financial logic to our thinking. He had the face of an intellectual fawn, a fine booming baritone, and a slender, wiry body that moved restlessly around the room as he analyzed business trends, production, population, growth, employment and cycles. I quarreled with him only about statistics, although he understood them and I didn't. "You think statistics are digits and zeros. I know they are people." Carl grunted tolerantly.

The economic ideas of James Harvey Rogers, Sterling Professor of Gold at Yale, disturbed me. He asked me to read Pareto, whom he admired. I looked into Volume I, and saw that I hadn't the background to profit from it. Pareto talked about elites and residues. His theories were the rationale for

Mussolini's activities. I disliked and feared his fascist philosophy. Rogers was no fascist, but I could not imagine what part of Pareto he liked.

Professor Warren Persons, shy and modest, was another constant economics mentor. Persons was a pioneer in measuring the growth of our country's economy. His imaginative approach and scientific methods would have been valuable in today's disturbed economy.

I used to watch the wives during long evenings of discussion on a high level of economic abstraction. But their thoughts were hidden. Every well-bred woman knew how to look understanding and interested when men of authority talked. Certainly women were assumed to be financial illiterates. Many didn't know their husband's income. They were given an allowance, or spending money. Money was a kind of Christmas present. It was a symbol of love designed by men.

I knew how much Eddie earned, because I was his partner in public relations, and ours was a joint bank account. But I didn't feel that I owned half the money, or any of it. The money, I felt, and still feel, belongs to him, and it is generous of him to let me use it for myself.

Many women were novices in the art of possessing and spending money. They were *nouveaux riches,* whether or not they had profited by inflation, whether or not their husbands were rich or poor, whether or not they had husbands or were self-propelled. They, too, spent suddenly and too lavishly. A short time before they had been told exactly how much to spend by the family wage earner. They were just emerging financially from their cocoons.

Few women at that time thought seriously about the relationship of spending and earning to the broad economic picture. Thekla, Eddie's cousin, was a brilliant exception. Her brother, Charles Augustus Bernays, had left the family fortune to her, and she became an expert in financial matters to guard the funds for her nieces and nephews. Her discussions on economics with Eddie were lucid, penetrating, and a warning to be financially awake—a warning I ignored, sadly.

It was Carl Synder who gave us the first forecasts of doom. Early in 1928 Carl said, "They're morons. They can't read the charts. They don't understand that the cycle of inflation is about to end. Eddie, liquidate your holdings."

Few were as far-sighted as Carl, and listening to him, I shuddered as I watched people grab their winnings and toss them around. Economists disagreed with one another and developed passionate theories on the duration of inflation. Tension, excitement and pleasure were paralleled in opposite directions by the anger, exasperation and despair of our wise economic friends. I am temperamentally pessimistic without any knowledge, so I backed Carl's predictions. Eddie, who is optimistic, objective and logical, got out of the market in the beginning of 1929. He urged his manic friends to bring down their balloons.

The great stock market crash of October 1929 stunned the entire financial world. American prosperity started its great slide downward. In a few days people started to look worried, or frightened. Angry. Sick. People who had believed their prosperity belonged to them. The wind blew out of inflation. As the months went on business men failed. Yachts were discarded, country homes closed, jewels and opera boxes sold. Unemployment started to develop into a great plague.

And yet a few people refused to believe that the crash was more than a stock market flurry, as one banker described it to Eddie. The depression deepened, unemployment increased, old dresses were refurbished. Housewives started thinking of themselves as unemployed, and men with jobs identified themselves fearfully with apple venders. Lines at soup kitchens rivaled lines at employment bureaus, but soup was more plentiful than jobs.

Roosevelt became President and declared a bank holiday in an exhilarating and radical attempt to halt the destruction of our economy. Carl and Rogers, unduly worried about public reaction to this dramatic measure, begged us to take our children away from Washington Square. "Union Square meetings might overflow. Possibly riots and brickbats. If I were you," said Carl, "I'd take my babies right out of town."

Eddie and I, scared for the children, rented a small house in Woodmere, L.I., by telephone, and in a few hours were on our way with Doris and Anne and four exuberant maids who took the word holiday literally.

Everyone took holiday as a cue. They beamed with pleasure and optimism. Debtors were going to stop tossing themselves from windows. Roosevelt had plugged up the bottom of the financial pit, and it was going to fill very quickly. Food shops cheerfully gave credit to housewives. Except the A & P chain stores, whose public resented its strict cash policy, its implied lack of faith in America's future.

We stayed in Long Island for a sheepish month, and returned to Washington Square disillusioned about the social wisdom of economic experts. Doris and Anne had enjoyed country life, Eddie had hated commuting, and I had loved living near Edith Barnett, a stimulating and selfless friend.

The financial crisis passed but the depression dug in for many grim years. Countless people walked the streets and highways for jobs, lay on subway gratings for fetid warmth, slept at library reading tables, froze on park benches and lined their shoes with newspaper. Malnutrition and exposure were the discreet words used to describe what people died of.

I developed a sense of guilt about money and possessions that still hurts me when I see shoes advertised at thirty-eight dollars a pair. I used to lie awake at night in Washington Square, mentally fitting beds into our rooms. Dormitories for the homeless. Shopping expeditions were masochistic excursions. I trudged through shops with a household list but hated everything I saw. The only things I could buy with a free conscience were for my children. They were exempt from the overshadowing frustration. When I ordered food for dinner parties I had to blindfold my super-ego to avoid figuring out how many people might have been fed how many days on one meal's budget.

How could any person with an adequate living escape a feeling of guilt, while millions of people shivered on bread lines? Apples, the symbol of desperation, were eaten as medicine for the conscience.

Children began to distrust evidences of wealth. They disapproved of people who did luxurious things. My daughter Dorie said, "I don't think people should go to school in automobiles. It's too noble." Her sister Annie backed her up, "Jane's sister has a fur coat, and she's only fifteen. Isn't that awful?" Doris asked me what bread lines were. After I had explained cautiously, she said, "Don't worry, Mommy. We'll take care of you and Eddie in your old age." My daughters and most of their friends still feel it is unkind and vulgar to dress better than their friends do, to ride in Pullman cars when there are day coaches, or to take taxis instead of subways and buses. Many of today's young people are haunted by the ghosts of depression bread lines they were too young to have seen.

Hitler drowned the depression in blood. Suddenly industry boomed in war preparation, derelicts turned into respected workers, products grew scarce, and taxes destroyed the comfortable faith that possessions were hereditary genes.

Discussions about taxes were toxic. "What's the use of working if you can't leave it to your children?"

"Taxes take all the incentive away. What's the use of working if it's taxed away?"

"Inheritance taxes are just plain socialism."

"How can you balance the budget if you spend so much on frills? Taxes go for frills."

That is the sort of conversation one used to hear. After two decades or so, people who talk of taxes still grumble, it is true. But their rationalization for hating to be taxed is somewhat less irrational. They have not yet achieved the realistic detachment of Benjamin Franklin: "In this world nothing can be said to be certain, except death and taxes."

Economics was forced out of the limelight by war work and war news. But price control, rationing and black markets brought out a good deal of latent human nature. We watched a prominent local politician alienate his constituency by giving a too lavish cocktail party, but Elsa Maxwell apologized for serving roast beef at a dinner party at the Waldorf Astoria. Rising a short way to her feet, she said, "In fairness to this hotel, to Mr. Boomer," smiling in his direction, "and to myself, I want to explain that this meat was cut from a steer sent me by a friend who owns a ranch." Her guests were mollified and reassured.

Gertrude Lawrence, in her dressing room after her performance in *Lady in the Dark,* talked contemptuously of "women in long dresses who don't seem to realize the danger we are in." We discussed raising funds for Britain.

In January, 1951, a renewed threat of inflation began to frighten the country. Inflation shared conversational honors with the Bomb, Acheson and Red China. At a dinner party an economist and a banker offered cures between spoonsful of Cherries Jubilee. "It's simple to halt inflation. Raise interest rates, increase taxes, and stop spending money on New Deal projects," said one economist. A businessman suggested, "I could stop inflation in a week by letting farm products find their own level. Farmers are terribly rich. If we don't, the middle class that depends on interest, pensions and the like will be wiped out." "Plow the farmer under?" I asked.

Eddie tried from time to time to explain financial matters to our daughters; the stock market, dividends, interest, shares that split, investment for profit, accumulations, gifts to social institutions, spending for pleasure. But he was rebuffed, politely enough.

I tried to reassure him. "Either they will learn when they have to, or they won't learn and there is nothing you can do about people who refuse to learn. Your daughters are intelligent because you taught them how to think. They'll be all right."

A few of my daughter's freshman classmates at Radcliffe were talking to me one day. "I hate to cash a check," said one of them. "She certainly does," said her friend. "She was so hard up last week she had to skip all her lunches, nearly starved to death." They all admitted, boasted or complained that they hated to draw out their own money. But they all reversed charges on telephone calls home.

"My mother said she didn't want me to charge things any more. 'You have a checkbook,' she scolded. 'Use that or pay cash.' So I said to her, 'but if I charge it, it's your money. If I pay cash, it's mine.' "

"Boys aren't as silly as that," said Mary smugly, as the argument speeded up. "At least they have a philosophy about money by the time they leave college."

"What is it?" we asked skeptically.

"Well, for one thing, they don't expect to be millionaires. Horatio Alger is dead. They don't look forward to keeping up with the Joneses because the Joneses aren't keeping up either."

"What do they want?" I asked.

"They want a good life. Security, leisure, broad interest, fun. They don't want success, necessarily. Any good job that they like is a good job. They don't have to be president of the company to feel right. They don't want any of that sort of status."

Our daughter Doris is, it would seem, starting to learn something about the relationship of money to the things she needs. She telephoned from Cambridge one day and casually said, "By the way, Mommie, Dick and I are thinking of buying a house. With some other people."

"What other people?"

"Some of the kids. You know."

I'm afraid I jibbered a bit at this point. I asked her if they were incorporating. Or if they knew anything about co-operative apartment houses. How, I asked, was she going to go about buying it?

She answered, "Oh, we're just going to the owner's lawyer and buy it."

"Well, you'd better talk to your father," I said and she answered, in some relief, I think, "That is what we want."

That was the beginning of two weeks of daily talks between New York and Cambridge. Eddie sent them to a highly respected law firm that consented to act for them.

Dorie called me up after the interview with the lawyer and said, "I wore a hat. I thought it would make me look responsible."

"What did the lawyer think?" I asked.

"He couldn't quite understand it," she told me. As a result six assorted incipient professors bought three-fourths of an acre in the heart of Cambridge and live happily in a house built for President Charles W. Eliot.

There is no point in trying to generalize about monetary attitudes of young people, just as it is pointless to try to generalize about attitudes of septuagenarians. However, economists, sociologists, psychologists and amateurs like me do it constantly.

For instance, the banker who told Eddie, "College girls simply won't spend any money. I have a wealthy client who tears his hair because his daughter's deposit account grows and grows. 'What does she think I work so hard for? What does she think I give her money for?' "

Many men who understand finance find it difficult to understand the young adults whose attitude toward expenditure is basically sociological. In Dallas, for instance, they join the swift drive upward on the social economic ladder. All outward evidences of comparative success are highly desirable. High school students in that city swap labels ripped from clothing. A girl gains prestige if a Neiman-Marcus label is revealed when she flings back her coat at a football game.

In other communities a young person loses status if he consistently exceeds the general spending limit of his group. The son of an old and prosperous Boston family lived in a shabby apartment, rode the subway or walked to work like most of his friends who were not too prosperous as young musicians. Not, he felt, that they objected to his being richer than they. They knew quite well that his resources were far greater than theirs. And not that they were jealous. But somehow money must not be allowed to confuse the issue of personal esteem and friendship. He explained all this to me, laboriously but patiently. He wanted me to understand that this was not social-political equalitarianism. He believed he was practicing good social psychology, and he was aware that individual economic attitudes are also bound up with the entire personality.

Money, for one thing, is predominantly a sex matter. Not in the Kinseyan sense, but in the societal and practical sense. Finance and Money on the grand level are male. Small moneys are female. This is based on male thinking, on female complaisance, on tradition and continuous conditioning. It is only in the past few years that the dividing line between feminine and masculine money has begun to smudge here and there.

Women have learned something about money, its limitations and advantages, with the encouragement of universities, banks and brokerage firms, because so much of the wealth of the land is in the name (sometimes confused with hands) of women. Many courses are given specifically for this new group of investors.

My few financially-minded friends feel that I betray all women by admitting that I will have nothing to do with investments. We have made a clear distribution of labor in our family. Eddie supervises the income and I limit the outflow.

Let my men, in my lifetime, stick to this last.

The failure of our society to recognize that women are part of our financial structure hurts the morale of men as well as women.

Our economic life is schizophrenic and will remain so until we are cured of our unwillingness to face reality. There are still some men who believe that women are congenitally incapable of economic independence; they hate the necessity but welcome the result of their wives' and daughters' work outside the home. Such conflict of emotions is destructive to the unity and happiness of the family.

Industry itself has made very little progress in changing its attitudes or practices. Women do not get equal pay for equal work, or equal opportunity, or equal advancement. This is obviously true in all grades of occupation, from unskilled factory work, through white collar, up to the ranks of management. Compare the salaries of graduates of Barnard College and of Columbia University for the past ten years. Compare, too, the positions and types of jobs they are in. It is true of professions, from teaching to preaching.

Women have no entrée into some trades and organizations or even to professional graduate schools. Although the country needs engineers, and women are now urged to enter this career, few schools of engineering welcome women to their classes. Recurrent shortages of doctors make it little easier for women to gain admittance into medical schools, to get interneships in hospitals afterward, and to get appointments in hospitals as residents.

Although fashion and retail merchandising are feminine interests, the Harvard Business School trains men for executive jobs in these fields but does not admit women. It was nationwide news when a woman, Dorothy Shaver, was made President of Lord & Taylor, and when Bernice Fitz-Gibbon was put on the board of directors of Montgomery, Ward. Such bias, besides injuring women and their families, creates competition that is unfair to men.

Our laws, too, suffer from a great time lag. Women are not permitted to transfer property in some states, or to make loans on their property. In a few states they may not own property; a husband is permitted to collect a woman's salary, and if he is a satyr, strip the clothes from her back.

Even taxation, the great leveler, handicaps women. A secretary is a deductible expense in business. But a woman who works to support her family is not permitted a deduction for a paid substitute worker in her home, an essential outlay, on which she must even pay a social security tax.

Half my life is professional. My work has measurable value. I am paid for my services. I am tangibly appreciated. In the amateur half of my life, I am not paid for my services. As a housewife I have no acknowledged value in this difficult and exacting profession that requires almost uncountable skills in execution and management for which I have not been trained.

Most damaging is the perpetuation of the contradictory idea that she is virtuous and praiseworthy to work as an amateur but that amateur housewifery is frittery, inefficient and suitable only for the inferior and peculiar mental level of women. In this ideological jungle, people run around in circles and arrive at a strange upside-down logic. Because housewives are wives and mothers and are all fine and admirable, therefore, nothing can surpass the value of the amateur to society.

We live in the age of the dominant amateur—in politics, in statesmanship, local, national and international, and even sometimes in industry. Men head vital endeavors for which they need have had no training, knowledge or liking. The principle that encourages parents to rear children without training is the same as the principle under which a Congressman, solely through priority, achieves chairmanship of a crucial committee.

The important activities of the world now slide along on natural wisdom and status, because amateurism has spread from the home to many fields of activity. Eddie questions the logic of the parallelism of professionalism and pay. Merely paying women won't make them professionals, and training them to be housewives, cooks and pedagogues won't ensure payment. He is right, of course. But I am convinced that there is an iron bond between training and professionalism, and between professionalism and monetary reward.

But who will pay wives for services they have always contributed to the moral, spiritual and physical welfare of their family? The complexity of devising any system for paying wives is staggering. Who *will* pay them? The husband whose budget is limited? The state? Society, that vague concept?

Who is subtle and wise enough to figure out a scale of payment, just and practical? Can cybernetics work out some correlation between a husband's changing earning power, a wife's years of service, her efficiency, her functions, and divide them by love?

A strong academic argument in favor of establishing a financial background for housewives is our embittering, degrading, and often confiscatory system of alimony. Some men are forced to support two or three ex-wives for many years. A ruthless woman can legally ruin a divorced husband. If, however, a reservoir of credit were built up for wives, men might live in relaxation with their latest mate. This was a flippant note in a discussion which ended on a tragic theme.

Grace, a gentle soul, took out her handkerchief and wiped her eyes. "When Jack asked for a divorce I refused alimony. It was too sordid. I just said he could pay for the four children's school and college. I'm looking for a job, but it's twenty years since I last worked."

There was an uncomfortable moment. Someone said

quickly, "I feel most sorry for elderly widows. They have a tough time because they have no sense of comparative values, they have no training in money matters. Suddenly they find themselves having to make decisions. When their husbands die they feel abandoned; they seem to have a picture of a poorhouse before them."

No matter how much or how little money widows have, they are frightened of their financial future. Even my mother, whose family was completely devoted, was occasionally, I am sure, afraid she would starve in spite of adequate dividends. When she was eighty-eight years old she went to the crowded millinery center on West 35th Street to buy parts which she assembled as really pretty hats for herself. I admired her black toque one day, and she said in timid triumph, "Oh, do you like it? Lina wants to buy one if I'll make it for her. Of course I'll make it. I can't let her pay, can I?"

Why is it that large sums of money are not as real as cash to any of us? A check is a piece of paper, but a quarter is two bits. It's tangible. Probably many of us are infantile, not far from the stage when we spent pennies, and Mother took care of everything else. Perhaps we feel that the bank takes care of everything but our minor spending money. The perpetuation of allowance-for-pleasure, to be carefully spent, while large sums are vague purchase symbols.

"I like realists, but I can't bear people who think money is a hard fact," said a successful playwright one evening.

A rough and tumble argument was on.

"How can anybody know when money is a fact, a symbol, an illusion or a delusion?"

"A nickel for a stick of chewing gum is a fact."

"Is it power or is it a symbol of power when a man uses it to buy power?"

"If he lives simply and peacefully in the country and writes poetry, it is a symbol of nothing."

"It's certainly a symbol of status if you carouse around the Riviera."

"But not if you live in Charleston, South Carolina, where people look down on wealth."

Perhaps people do not understand symbols as well as they think they do. Money is status, or is it a symbol of status? And why, if money is a symbol of status, must there be so much displacement of symbols? You can have a million dollars, but you've also got to have the electric dishwasher, or the air-conditioned Cadillac, or the Dior gown, to prove that money and status are equal to each other. Which, of course, they aren't.

That is where illusion comes in and muddies the symbolism. Status and power function beautifully in America without wealth. Many of us mix up means with desire.

A modern investment adviser like John Richards talks to his clients last of all about the financial aspect of their funds. He insists on knowing first about his client's value system, about his aspirations, his obligations to others, his wishes for the near and distant future. Money to the client of a modern psycho-sociological financial adviser becomes mystic fuel for the magic carpet. Charity, scientific research, global mobility, sea voyages, retirement to a farm, leisure for hobby pursuits, college for his children, security for his wife? What do you want? Your savings can buy you all or none of these. Hold on to your social security.

"Aren't you talking about dichotomy?" asked Eddie.

"I suppose I am," I answered. "I think we have been deluded. We don't know the difference between reality and fantasy; we are neurotic about money. The conflict between our idealism and materialism is driving us nuts."

Who will teach our children these things? Parents are not very good teachers, I have found. Children are decidedly skeptical about adult standards and economic methods. They have heard too much about depressions. They believe they will learn from their own experiences and observations.

But experience is a poor economics teacher too. I think not irrelevantly of my nephew Martin, who got a job as a chore boy in a summer hotel in Maine when he was fourteen years old. His parents had mixed emotions as they watched him grin ingratiatingly when guests tipped him too liberally. Bea, his mother, said, "I think it's terrible. He makes as much as $45 a week. He is certainly being miseducated."

I have found that communism in Middle America, austerity in England, import duties on clocks, drought in the West —all these affect my life as a housekeeper. Food, clothing, implements and essential services are better or poorer because of events that seem far away from my refrigerator or my children's dress closets.

I think, too, of the mounting anxiety among experts over the innumerable debts of innumerable people who have been taught by business, through advertising and promotion, to want and purchase too many things that are not justified by their earning power.

Our educational system shares a good deal of responsibility for our ignorance. That is because colleges still hold to the medieval ideal of aloofness from life, and to the nineteenth-century idea that education is a cultural sugar-coating for the elite. Educators like Mrs. Millicent McIntosh, president of Barnard College, who are aware that life and learning must be brought closer together, find themselves struggling against the negative pulls of tradition.

Schools and colleges should assume the responsibility of teaching men and women their functions in an economic society. Doris and Anne escaped all instruction on economics during sixteen years of schooling. Through war shortages and after war upheavals they were allowed to stay ignorant of why red or blue shoes were unavailable. Later in their schooling they should have been taught their role as citizens who would vote for legislators responsible for the expenditure of money. They would someday influence questions of taxation, salaries for teachers, road building, farm subsidies and public health. Our system of government would be far stronger if more of us had been taught how to evaluate economic measures.

Boys and girls might well be taught technical matters, such as budgeting, as well as abstract study of economic systems. More important, they should be taught how to evaluate the importance of their wishes and needs, how to measure their present against the future, and, above all, how to appraise material yardsticks, emotional props and valid instruments of civilization.

CHAPTER FOUR

In Praise of Parents

Nature has made women more like children in order that they may better understand and care for children.

Havelock Ellis, *Man and Woman*

"You can count on only one thing about your children. Whatever you do for them will be wrong," said my cousin, who has a large albumful of fine children and grandchildren to prove that her pessimism was unjustified. But in a major way she was right. Eddie and I became parents when our babies and the squalling sciences of child care and child psychology were new. We opened our arms wide to each new theory, believing that each latest one would solve all problems of bringing up children, and with equal enthusiasm we discarded old theories, believing they were quite wrong.

Everything we did for our children was condemned a few years later. I suspect that my generation of parents had the most confusing and difficult parental job of any generation in history since the Children's Crusades.

Starting with experimental kindergartners, we progressed to experimental psychologists, who were sure that we could train children to be nearly perfect by almost mechanical processes. When Freud hit the nursery our lives were made really complex. We had to check everything we did or didn't do with current pedagogic interpretations of psychoanalytic theories.

There have been complete revolutions in child care in the last few decades. The printing press and other means of communication have hurried new ideas into and out of public acceptance. I am sure of only one thing—there will be new theories and new methods every ten years.

I think if we as parents had not been amateurs, untrained and ignorant, we would not have been so vulnerable. We would, with confidence in our own judgment, have been able to stand up in the rushing white waters of psychology. We would have had a sense of comparative values and continuity.

Eddie and I were the first parents in the world. We did not then have a feeling for the mystic flow of human experience by which a child learns how to be a parent and as a parent learns about his own childhood by watching and listening to his children. Present and past in some measure lead to the future, but we cannot see what is around the next bend in the river.

Whether we think we are bringing up our children by the deceptive rule of common sense, as our grandparents did, or by the thoughtful advice of child-guidance experts, we have, all of us, been influenced by some philosopher whose abstract thoughts have come down to us from the past. Whatever we do is in some measure intellectually induced. We are merely iron filings, mysteriously pulled into neat patterns by the magnets of ideas.

It is a mistake to underestimate the power of philosophy. Although its effect may be delayed and indirect, eventually it may decide for us whether our children shall pick up their toys at the end of the day, or not, and in what way we shall show our love for them. The reasoning of a sixteenth-century philosopher may become a psychologist's theory in the nineteenth century. And this, in the early twentieth century, may become a rule of conduct. From Emerson and William James it is only a short line through John Dewey to the City and Country School on Twelfth Street where my children learned arithmetic by playing store.

Philosophy and religion were the main guides for our

grandparents in training their children. My friend, who is a great-grandfather himself, told me, "My Pop believed original sin meant inborn devilishness. He used to take me out to the barn every Saturday and beat hell out of me whether I had been bad or not." I was happy that beatings have never run in my family.

Our grandparents and parents had an easy time bringing up their children. All they had to do was to develop their character and make them wear long underwear. There was no child psychology and almost no pedagogy. Character building was simple and clear but they had to keep everlastingly at it. While their main emphasis was on character, we, as parents had to cope with psychology.

How hard it is to recall the events, frowns and scoldings by which my parents tried to give their children a proper attitude toward life. Moth brought us up in all the ways we take for granted, but Pop's special province was character, ethics and morality. I believe he thought our characters were good, with a few minor reservations. It would not have occurred to him to warn us not to cheat, lie, steal or murder.

His method was to take advantage of bad examples set by other people. He appraised other people with a scalpel in one hand and Oblivion at his feet. When the great Caruso pinched a lady in the Monkey House and shocked the entire civilized world, Pop consigned him to a special and spacious Oblivion and forbade me ever to mention his name again.

I rarely argued with Pop, but I ventured to wonder if perhaps there might not be some explanation for Caruso's strange crime. Pop looked at me icily. "There is no excuse. He is a barbarian."

My father was an unworldly man. He was an idealist. He was a perfectionist, and I know he was perfect because my mother told us so. Pop believed that character was the pervasive texture of personality. Whatever your character was, everything you did was an expression of it. Character was something you were. You were, and therefore you did the right things. Character showed up especially when the going was hard, as if there ought to be a character reservoir inside you that you could count on in emergencies.

He believed, too, that you could choose your character, and it would be either black or white. He hoped, of course, that you would select goodness, honesty, kindness and the ideal attitude toward life. Character, I gathered, was slightly different from soul. Soul was a thing you had or didn't have. There was nothing much you could do about it.

Honesty was a great part of character. Who could forget Pop's reaction when he learned that a trade association was to present him with a grandfather's clock as a symbol of their esteem? "That would be a cheat," he said in shocked disapproval. "I am not a grandfather." Mother tried to persuade him to accept it, but he refused the grandfather crown thrice. I wondered if only grandfathers could have grandfather clocks, and asked, "It will be your grandchildren's grandfather's clock, won't it?" That made the clock honest and Pop yielded.

We learned quite young that perhaps honesty is not an absolute. Take the question of Christmas and Santa Claus. For a number of years my brother Leon and I were uncomfortable about the whole question. We knew that our parents were Santa, but we weren't quite sure of it, because Mother continued the myth. We put pins in the tops of our stockings in case there was a Santa who might have any idea of putting coals in for our sins. Somehow we knew the pins wouldn't stick our parents if they turned out to be Santa.

Remembering all this, and because I was dominated, and still am, by Pop's value judgments, I told our children a slightly gilded version of the truth when they were quite young. "You told us much too soon," said Anne. "It would have been fun to believe in Santa much longer."

Whatever the cause, my children are spectacularly honest.

I realized this when Anne came home from school and told me, "I am a rangaroo in the play and I am very cute."

Dorie, also disarmingly honest said, "I am the best runner in our class. Only so-and-so and so-and-so are faster." She named all the other children. Self-respect, accuracy and a nice sense of unreality combined to give her an all-around glow of happiness.

Pop had a few doubts about the perfection of our characters. But, looking back, I believe he included many things in morality that perhaps were not strictly part of the ethics department of life.

When I put dead-white rice powder on my nose—Elizabeth Arden's rainbow had not yet been invented—Pop lashed at me, "Wipe that powder from your nose. You look as if you had fallen into a flour barrel." It must have looked fairly grotesque against my sun-bronzed cheeks, streaked with tears. When Bea and I discovered that my aunt used rouge secretly, we couldn't reconcile the terrible deceit with her otherwise virtuous and gentle behavior.

Pop thought anything in bad taste was sinful, like giggling or an unbecoming hat. Vulgar people or vulgarity of any kind were unforgivable. Tennis was virtuous, particularly on extremely hot days. Pop built tennis courts wherever he rented a summer cottage. Moth stood at the sideline, pleading, "Sam, stop playing. Sam, it's too hot. Doris, you stop then." But Pop was a stoic. The hotter it was, the longer he played. I knew how he felt and admired his courageous character as he ran about, a small slender man with a fluffy fringe of white hair around his sun-reddened scalp.

Riding a high front-wheel bicycle was virtuous, too. I can remember following him about, watching him pick himself up every time he fell from the asymmetrical machine and laboriously mount it again. Here was significant determination that withstood scraped knees and an affront to his own sense of decorum.

Pop judged character even by one's conversation. My sister Beatrice, with the face of an angel, was 'way ahead of me in adjustment, although she was three years younger than I. She had an uncanny understanding of what people wanted and a tact that charmed Pop. At supper on East 48th Street, in the homey dining room facing the street, as we progressed from soup to roast to pie, she kept the conversation going with pleasant little stories about her friends. My approach was tactless. I could never understand why Pop resisted my efforts to change his convictions. Mother would start with a small conversational sortie:

"Did you read about the bank clerk who absconded with $100 yesterday, Sam?"

Pop summed it up: "Scoundrel."

"Maybe he wasn't a scoundrel," I might offer rashly. "Maybe he had to support a lot of children and an invalid wife and he didn't have enough . . ."

"Don't argue," said Pop, and I became a little child again. That, of course, was the most incomprehensible part of growing up. I was like the frog, up one jump and down two, up five and back one.

Grandpa and our favorite uncle thought it was their special duty to save Bea and me from vanity. Uncle Isaiah, who was very handsome, used the device of saying to me, "If I had a face like yours, I'd go jump in the lake."

"Look in the mirror and tell me what you see," he commanded Bea. She looked and answered, "Me."

"No," he corrected her gravely. "You see a monkey." Bea cried and has scarcely forgiven him in a half century.

Grandpa cautioned me, "Don't look in the mirror or it will crack." Or, "If you make such a face, it will freeze that way if the clock strikes twelve."

We knew Grandpa and Uncle I were fooling, but we believed them.

Our own children developed their own characters. Eddie

and I never worried about their being sinful, or even delinquent. We had psychology to worry about and that kept us quite busy.

A mother's duties fit neatly in one short paragraph. She must feed, clothe and keep her baby warm, and develop its personality, its feeling of security, build its character, give it education and recreation and teach it to be a social being in the broad and good meaning of the word.

Taking care of the physical needs of your child is comparatively easy. Teething, vaccinations, stomach-aches and twisted ankles are painful but fleeting. Scraped beef and pureed vegetables soon give way to whole food. Running after a scampering child is no harder than chasing a tennis ball.

It is the intangibles that fill your mind and your spare minutes. Your own emotional attitudes toward your child, the important and subtle relationships within your family—these are matters of wonder and study, of occasional sleepless nights, of goose-pimples and, generally, of delight. These are the most lasting and rewarding of your scheduled duties as a mother.

Although our parents and grandparents were fussy about our character, they were quite autonomous about showing their love for us. They did not have to worry about showing their feelings for us. Love was no problem at all; it was a pleasure. It was only in our troubled generation that affection for children became controversial.

Grandpa showered us with affection, as most grandfathers would like to do if they were allowed to. He sang to me as I sat on his lap, and the stories he told me of his childhood were, I think, more exciting than westerns are to today's children, perhaps because they had really happened to him. He told me how as a young boy in 1839 he had sailed on a ship that was battered by a long line of catastrophes between Germany and America. Cholera broke out, passengers and crew got scurvy, and a hurricane tumbled water casks about and shattered them. Potatoes burst from their sacks and rolled around turbulent decks. Then he told me how he had played pool with General Grant in Galena, Illinois, and how his handsome brother, Ike, ran from a Confederate cannon ball that chased him up a hill.

My mother did not show affection often. I liked it very much when occasionally she cupped my chin in her warm hand. Pop despised any display of emotion. As a ritual, rather than an expression of emotion, we brushed their cheeks lightly with a kiss for good-bye, hello and good-night. Moth's cheek was soft and hot, but Pop's was cool, and more like a kid glove than a face. We never kissed good-morning.

Before Eddie and I became parents we were quite naïve about being affectionate to children. If anybody had asked us, we would have said that parental love is instinctual, biological, spiritual—altogether natural and pleasant. We had no idea that there were rules and that experts had decided to count a mother's kisses and measure a father's exuberant embrace.

We were warned that one caress too many might destroy our children's healthy adjustment to life. We listened and believed but we cheated constantly. When no one could see us we petted our babies as happily as any primitive, but we had to pet them in secret.

The babies' nurse terrified us, scolding bitterly, "Well, why don't you climb right into the bassinet with her?" It was not as if I were one of those loathsome cannibalistic mothers who eat their children in an excess of maternal hunger. I did not burden them with affection. If I had, they would have told me so, as Dorie did when she was four years old. "Kissing," she decided, "is e-nauseating."

Under the stultifying influence of the love-austerity cult, Eddie was inhibited for the first time in his life, and tried, without success, to hide his affection. He discussed children endlessly and objectively. At parties I could hear his words as counterpoint to other conversation—frustration, identification, sibling relationships. What he was really saying through all these words was, "Listen to the cute thing my baby did."

My seventeen-year-old nephew Martin explained to me, "I never liked kissing, so I gave a peck to Mom and a punch in the stomach to Dad. Kissing is smother love. Kissing can go with strictness and it can go with spoiling."

Today's parents are luckier. Child psychologists have invented T.L.C.—Tender, Loving Care and, perhaps unnecessarily, are trying to explain to women that love is wholesome, that it gives a child security and that it has real value for the personality. T.L.C. is prescribed nowadays for all kinds of emotional and physical ills as if parental affection were an extra ingredient in a formula: add smoothly and gently, a teaspoonful three times a day.

Science burst into the nursery when we were young parents and stirred our imaginations. If children were properly reared, we were told, future generations would be wise and good and unselfish.

I believe that dog trainers first made child psychology popular by interpreting Pavlov to the public. We became aware of dogs who dripped saliva when a bell rang even after food had been disassociated from it. We learned about conditioning, about the comparative merits of reward and punishment in the learning process.

Then came Dr. John B. Watson and his new doctrine of behaviorism. Eddie and I used to listen to him, fascinated by his theories, as we sat in the living room in Washington Square and our babies slept upstairs. We had no idea how quickly behaviorism would vanish from the psychological battle.

While behaviorism lasted, everybody whispered to babies and nobody dared to drop them because Watson had discovered the two basic fears—fear of noise and fear of falling.

Technical approaches and the jargon of psychology

crowded out all other topics of conversation. Self-expression, conditioned reflex, stimulus, these rang bravely through living rooms until newer ideas took over. Mother fixation and wishful thinking came in with subjective psychology and psychoanalysis.

Unfortunately, like many other parents and many teachers, we tried to work Freud backward. The pedagogy of the period was based on the notion that we could prevent children from developing neuroses later in life. Because Freud had shown that mental ills in adults were tied up with childhood damage, we believed, leaping from crag to illogical crag, that if we could guard our children against shocks and psychic wounds they would grow up well-adjusted and happy.

There were special dangers to watch out for. The Oedipus complex threatened little boys who were too attached to their mothers, and the Electra complex would harm little girls who remained too long attached to their fathers. But even the complex was not simple. We were also told that unless girls loved their father, and boys their mother, they would have difficulty later in loving their wife or husband. Heterosexual child love must be strong but not too strong if the husband-wife relationship is to be good. It was completely impossible to figure this out. I decided finally that the more my daughters loved their father the happier we all would be.

Another danger signal which sent us diving into the nearest book on child psychology was a child's overdependence. When Doris was three-and-a-half she was interviewed for admission to the City and Country School. Carolyn Pratt's grimaces and her unanswerable questions terrified Dorie, who hid her face in my neck for safety. Miss Pratt said, "Clearly she has a mother fixation. You'd better do something about it."

I consulted my friend Dr. A. A. Brill, who gave me the shortest psychoanalysis on record. He smiled and said, "Wean her and get her a dog. A smooth-haired dog. A bulldog. A

Boston Bull." I bought a long-haired dog, a golden cocker spaniel. Now married, Dorie is notably devoted to her husband, her job and her home in Cambridge.

All through history, all over the world, parents have tried to keep their children from being afraid. But methods of developing fearlessness keep changing. In my childhood we were so ashamed of being afraid that we were helpless. No one helped us conquer fear because nobody knew we were afraid.

I lived next door with Aunt Rose for a few days when my parents were still at the seashore. Aunt Rose asked me to get a few towels from our dark and vacant house. I couldn't tell her I was afraid. As I slowly climbed the dark stairs I thought I heard the measured tread of my own doom. When, as parents, we suspected our children were afraid of the dark, we kept a light burning for them.

Mothers should be skilled in mental telepathy so that they can sense the strange fears of children.

My daughter at the age of fifteen said, "Do you know why I was so scared when the doctor pricked my finger?" I wanted very much to know.

She continued, "I used to think he was drinking my blood through the tube."

"Why didn't you let me wash behind your ear when you were a child?" I asked.

"Oh, that," she said. "I thought the hole from my mastoid went right into my head."

Half my life as a mother was devoted to trying to prevent my children from developing a sense of fear. The other half was spent trying to prevent myself from being afraid for them. When your child puts a hairpin in an electric outlet and the odor of her burned hand fills the room, your fear is mingled with fury at the man who placed this lethal outlet near the floor.

To prevent unnecessary anxieties, I previewed any motion

picture that I was to take them to. *Snow White* I thought was terrifying, but because all their friends went, it seemed necessary for Annie and Dorie to see it. I warned them in advance and poked fun at the horror spots. Nevertheless, Annie shivered normally at the dreadful witch. As if art were a horse that she ought to remount after being thrown, I took her to *Snow White* again next week and she sat through it without a qualm. I was proud of my tremendous accomplishment.

"Don't let your child be an introvert," was another warning to parents. There was an adult compulsion to make children do and act, to race, to run, to read, even to relax in a dynamic way. "Now lift your hand, now let it fall and be soft," the teacher at City and Country School told the children.

We had national introvertophobia. Daydreaming was *verboten*; it might lead to schizophrenia. Idleness was a crime. If you act fast and continuously you will conform, you will be adjusted, you will have no time to stray or to wish for a change, or, worse still, imagine that there might be a change.

We Freudian parents had to beware of so many psychic dangers that bringing up our children was like running an obstacle race. We had to make sure they were not suppressed. ("Let them yell, it's good for them to make a noise.") They mustn't be given an inferiority complex, that most common affliction. ("Oh, my, that's a beautiful picture. Tell me all about it.") We tried to guard them from getting a sense of guilt. ("You couldn't help breaking the pitcher. Someone put it too near the edge.") Of course all these problems were worked out on a child's level; it obviously could not be done on a level of maturity. You couldn't help your child on the level of international politics. Sin was suddenly lifted from our children's slender shoulders and placed on our own burdened back. If children weren't wicked somebody had to be; therefore, it was the parents. If they refused to go to bed it was our fault.

If Freud changed our over-all attitude toward children, Dewey turned our concept of discipline upside down. The whole idea of discipline is as unstable as a drop of mercury on a lazy susan. I have seen the strict discipline of my father ("Yes, sir") give way to full permissiveness ("When can we stop doing whatever we want to?"). In recent years there has been a return to the back-of-the-hand and do-what-I-say-immediately approach.

My mother was strict about clean underwear and hair-brushing; but instead of telling us, she nagged in the fashion of the day. I don't know whether she was too busy or too soft-hearted to discipline us. At any rate, I didn't go to kindergarten because I couldn't get myself dressed in time. Was she really too busy to help me or was she aiming to develop my independence? I do know that she attended the earliest meetings of the Child Study Association. I would give a good deal to know what they talked about, what they thought were the problems, and whether they had any answers to them.

My father kept us in uneasy subjection by lowering the temperature of his blue eyes. Eddie's father was a famous disciplinarian. Every evening one of his children stood sentry duty to warn the rest that they saw his jaunty figure coming up the avenue, swinging a cane. "Papa's here," the look-out yelled and all the children ducked. They seemed to fear him long after they were grown.

Eddie's Uncle Sigmund, whom I visited in Vienna not long after I was married, asked me, "How do you get along with Eddie's father?" "Fine," I answered. "He is always delightful and I like him very much." "Aren't you afraid of him? Doesn't he yell as he used to?" I tried to explain. "I can leave the room when he is cross because I am not his child." Freud nodded agreement.

Discipline is as vague a word as you can find in the whole vocabulary of human conduct. It can mean anything from a gentle "No, no," to a policeman's bullet. It can mean rigid external regulations, or sympathetic encouragement of inner control.

When my first daughter was born discipline was associated with habit formation. It started in the maternity hospital's nursery. Infants were permitted to cry so that they would learn that crying did no good. If you picked them up, they would learn to demand constant attention by crying. I believe this was a device to make life easier for baby nurses. During the first few days of Dorie's life, nurses tried to instill in her the habit of being very considerate. They may have been right, but this kind of discipline was too hard on me and I quickly rebelled.

Everything in Dorie's infancy was planned for her by experts who knew infallibly at what time of the day and night she would be hungry, when to the minute she would want to play, when she would want to sleep, in what month she would sprout her first tooth, when she would start to crawl backward, when she would take her first step. She was slave to a stop watch. Nothing mattered but time. She was kissed on time, she was bathed on time, she was exercised on time. She might cry fit to break my heart but the clock might refuse to let me feed her. Demand feeding came twenty years too late for me. I would, with great pleasure, have let my babies ring their own dinner bells. As a teen-ager Doris was quite contemptuous of time but I cannot deduce any cause-and-effect relationship.

By the time Anne was born only a year and a half later, discipline, rules and stop watches were falling into disrepute. Experts had discovered that a child's world is different from an adult world. Adults had to learn the dimensions of a child's world.

I loved the idea. I wanted to know what would make my children comfortable and happy. Mentally I threw away last year's textbooks. I practiced empathy, sympathy, forgiveness and indulgence. I became permissive. If the children wanted candy before dinner I let them choose the pieces they wanted. If they, somewhat later, of course, wanted to play with matches I showed them how to do it and where, stipulating only that an adult be there.

I felt that children ought to know that parents are people. I tried to show them that I was often wrong, and that their ideas were worth consideration. I felt my superior size and age gave me an unfair advantage over them. Parenthood, it seemed to me, carried too much power.

Permissiveness blew into my life, cool and comforting as the trade winds in the tropics. This, too, was based on reading Freud backward. If you were permissive you didn't scold or punish your child. My main task was to encourage the limpid flow of their personality. This was logical to me because I had always thought children naturally wanted to be good, pink and wise. Certainly my children did. They learned to behave because they liked to imitate people they admired.

I liked not scolding them but sometimes it was a little difficult to make a point without punctuation. When Annie spilled milk, which she hated, she felt sorry enough without a scolding. I commiserated with her, "There, there, it's all right, don't worry." Anne now tells me she wouldn't have felt nearly so badly about the spilled milk if I had yelled at her. The entire question of preserving the child's personality is exceedingly bewildering. At any rate, Annie still hates milk, and I agree that milk tastes like rubber.

I may have carried permissiveness too far. Anne, now married, said, "You always used to say, 'Wouldn't you like to pick up your toys?' I thought you knew I wouldn't like to. I wanted you to say, 'Do it,' or 'You must do it.' "

When Dorie was five years old, I took her to the opera to see the wedding of Lohengrin and Elsa because she loved brides. She leaned over the railing trying to get closer to the stage. A woman in the next box hissed at her, "Sit back, you'll fall," and glared at me. People constantly tried to take care of my children when I seemed to ignore the peril they were in at any moment.

Even Pueblo Indians are permissive parents. My friend Adele Franklin, Dorie, Annie and I spent a summer visiting villages around Santa Fe. We found that discipline started only at the age of puberty when a child became a responsible adult.

At a corn festival, noisy and crowded with tourists, a little boy cried in terror, as I judged by the sound of his voice. After a few minutes his father took him by the hand and led him into their adobe home.

"Is his father going to wallop him?" someone asked.

"No," said Adele, "the little boy will just have to stay in there until he stops crying. Crying is the only offense for which a child is punished."

Psychiatrists are now raising hell with permissiveness. They say with authority that some discipline gives a child a sense of security. Talking about this with a psychologist, I said that I was sad about this reversion to discipline. She looked at me disdainfully and guessed, "You were a permissive parent." She added, "I bet you were afraid of your children, too."

"I still am afraid of them," I admitted, "and so is Eddie."

My children, now grown up, agree with her. Annie said to me, "Mommie, you weren't strict enough with us. I'm going to be very strict with my children." I suspect that may not be her final idea on the subject.

It is all very confusing. Especially since theory in the abstract may be interpreted in any number of ways in day-to-day conduct. You may believe in discipline but you may also be too tender-hearted to enforce it. You may believe in gentle and thoughtful handling, but you may be so tired that you are impatient and irritable.

Often it is the extra-maternal duties—making beds, washing diapers, marketing—that make you yearn for a long vacation. Overwork can thin the edge of your voice. Your sweet disposition and wisdom are sometimes swept out with the rubbish. You can only hope that your baby is intuitive enough to know that love lies behind your irascibility.

I don't believe my generation of parents paid more attention to sex education and sex problems than parents in the Elizabethan age, or in the Reconstruction era or in Victoria's day, even though Freud was thought to have invented the subject.

Sex is an omnibus word like rheumatism and traffic. It covers a great many ideas, from procreation to occupation. When I was a child in the 1890's the differences between boys and girls were mainly matters of strength, behavior and clothes, not libido. We knew vaguely that sex and gender were not synonymous.

I knew boys were dangerous but wonderful. Their play was rough. Their snowballs were hard, even without stones in the center. They made us play sentry on cold evenings until our feet nearly froze. They teased viciously. They were godlike but cruel, in an Old Testamentary way. My brother Leon set the pattern and I still feel that men must be placated.

We always knew about procreation, as most children have through the ages. No one had to tell us. Our back yard was as educational as a farm. Mating was a natural, if rather grotesque behavior of animals, but it had no resemblance to sex in the Hollywood-oriented minds of today's children. Cats gave us kittens to cherish, and dogs had puppies for us to play with. We couldn't quite understand why parents liked to be mysterious about such obvious matters.

I tried to tell my mother that I knew about such things, but the effort was deeply painful to both of us.

"Moth, I know about babies," I said as she stood warming her back at the hot-air register. Moth's face turned deep red. After a while I went away.

A few years ago—when she was eighty-four and I was fifty-eight—she told me she too Knew About Such Things when she was supposed to be innocent about Life.

"When I was twelve years old," said Moth, "Katie, our upstairs girl, told me she was going to have a baby. It was all the fault of a workman in the lumber yard, and would I please help her? She wanted me to talk to the man and try to make him do something for her. I nearly died just to think of such a thing. Of course I couldn't talk to the man. So Katie fell downstairs purposely. After the miscarriage she came back to our house and stayed with us for years."

"What did Grandma say?" I asked.

"My parents didn't know. I couldn't possibly talk to *them* about such a thing."

When my children were small the general educational climate convinced us that we should tell our children everything. Enlighten your children about sex, said Freudians, so that they may not learn the facts shockingly and improperly. This made some sense to me. My children lost all interest in anything I told them about sex in answer to their questions. When Dorie asked, "How are babies born?" I told her. She pondered for a few seconds and then asked the next question, "What I can't understand is what makes the telephone bell ring when someone calls you." We spared our children the euphemisms and confusions of the birds-bees-and-flowers period of sex education.

There has been a complete change in our attitude toward the body. In the early part of this century physical growth was shameful. My body matured under layers of clothes that screened femininity because its evidence was taboo. Our bras were tight corset-covers that camouflaged nature. I remember a straight-lined white pique dress that was one year too young for me when I was thirteen years old. It showed faintly that I was no longer a flat-chested child, and to hide the revelation I walked with shoulders curved forward. When Moth insisted, "Stand up straight," she could not have known the impelling reason for my bad posture.

Biological processes were carefully concealed. No one talked about any of the functions of the human machine, except eating and sleeping. I learned painfully why girls needed regularly to invent colds and sore throats. We wore, too often, sprained-wrist bands or sprained-ankle straps to explain why we weren't playing tennis or swimming. My children, casually admitting natural anatomical functions, were spared such needless subterfuges and embarrassments.

I talked to them candidly about dangers, too, when they were so young that they needed to be warned. I explained to Dorie, "Sometimes you get separated from the other girls and their mothers at the movies, don't you?" She nodded. "Well, sometimes a man sitting next to you may bother you—stroke your arm or leg, or something. If that happens, don't make a fuss, just get up and quietly go to another seat."

A few months later Dorie said gleefully, "It happened, what you told me about. This afternoon."

"What happened?" I asked.

"You know. The man next to me squeezed my knee." She grinned.

"Did you move to another seat?" I asked.

"I did not," she answered emphatically. "There was no other good seat. I just took off my class pin and stuck him in his knee, and he got up and went away."

I never worried about her sex life after that.

I have had to cope with the damning fact that my children at the age of sixteen knew more about sex than I did at thirty-two. No subject was taboo, no branch of biology shied at. They knew all about sex in its narrowest and in its cosmic implications. They knew many long words like emotional response, nymphomania and homosexuality. But I am not sure that they understood the meanings.

Anne was a senior at the Brearley School when the Kinsey

report on *Sexual Behavior in the Human Male* came out. She read it for days and then asked me if she might take it to school to show to the other girls. She quickly agreed that the girls' parents might be shocked.

Certainly up to a point there was a great candor between my generation and our children. Annie whispered to me one day when her good friend Jane was playing a Chopin waltz with astonishing fury, "She's having mother trouble, that's why she's playing so loud." Jane smiled apologetically, got up from the piano and said, "I'd rather not talk about it because, after all, you're a mother, too, and you'd have to take her side." Ten minutes later, between mouthfuls of cheese soufflé, Jane was unburdening her emotions.

"Look, did you ever interfere with Anne's friends—I mean if you disapproved of them?"

"I might, under certain conditions."

"I mean," said Jane, "if Anne went with a girl you disapproved of because that girl behaved in a way you thought was bad [this was delicacy in word choice in deference to my age], would you say, 'No, you can't go with her because people will think you are bad because you're her friend?"

"Mommy, you know what she means," explained Annie. "You know you never really stopped me from going with you-know-who because she slept with boys."

Such candor is often staggering to a parent. Nevertheless the moral revolution of the last few decades presents such enormous responsibility and difficulty for young people that I felt the only helpful thing a mother could do was to explain the truth as she knew it, to have courage and to stand by.

Some conversations are shattering. When Annie was eighteen and more sophisticated than she is now at twenty-five, she said to me, "I'm glad you like Fanny. She's such fun. She loves to make boys think she's not a virgin but of course she wouldn't think of sleeping with anyone."

I was fascinated. "How does she make them think she's not a virgin?" I asked.

"By flirting and acting sexy. She puts on an act. She gets a great kick out of it. By the way, she says I'm the only girl she knows besides herself that's really a virgin."

I told this story to Eddie but he couldn't see anything funny in it. Perhaps I didn't tell it right. But I think it revealing to hear the new attitude toward sexual morality summed up so innocently, and probably incorrectly. Boys have habitually bragged about imaginary sex achievements. For centuries wayward girls have tried to conceal any lapse from virtue. Today boys and girls seem to be sitting on the same side of the turntable.

Morality by definition is a matter of custom. Whatever the social standards, conformity is a matter of life or death to a child. There is nothing quite so poignant as the shame and loneliness of being different. When all children carry toy pistols, no peace-loving mother can, with impunity, forbid her child the pleasures of murder. My daughters said they couldn't possibly wear leggings to school, no matter how icy the weather. "All the girls wear short socks." I agreed and shivered in the wind.

Parents at the turn of the century did not have to choose between conformity and what was good for us. They were the same thing. We were trained like carriage horses. Every day a new high was added to our check-reins: Sunday School, dancing school, thank-you notes, calling cards, white kid gloves for matinees, curtseys to guests, "Yes, sir" to Pop, never contradict, stand for your elders.

"Put your hat on straight," said Pop, looking up from Spencer. "Only chippies wear their hats tilted. Where are you going? Walking on Broadway? Ladies don't walk on Broadway." I was sixteen years old. Our Broadway promenade was between 107th Street, where we lived, and 96th Street. This was our Main Street and we paraded, bowing sedately to the young men we knew, who paraded merely for the pleasure of tipping their hats to us. Girls walked with girls and boys with boys. This custom is still in vogue in Guatemala where brightly dressed Indians stroll about the square of Chichicastenango, girls going clockwise and men the other way, or vice-versa. I think it is a pleasant way of stimulating the hormones.

Conformity, I admit, has certain values. It is a support, a crutch in new situations and occasionally it has life-saving properties. My daughter Anne made history in New Mexico by riding down a steep arroyo, hands and feet in the air calling gleefully to Slim, our infuriated guide, "Look what I can do."

My father was especially interested in the negative aspects of conformity, or what we call censorship today. When I was quite young our reading was not censored at all. Father had no idea that children's books could be harmful. Most of my reading as a child was done in bed by the feeble rays of light that passed over the transom of the folding doors between the front room, where Pop and Moth were reading, into the back room where I was supposed to be sleeping. Today it is practically impossible for me to read sitting up.

Much of my reading was done in the Public Library at 58th Street and Lexington Avenue and I have a warm memory of the low comfortable chairs and tables in the children's room.

Sometimes the books we were allowed to read were not altogether harmless. *The Wizard of Oz* and Poe's stories served to lengthen my prayers to include every possible catastrophe from cyclones to earthquakes. I read every available fairy-tale and enjoyed their horrors. Not many years later fairy-tales were placed on the black-list by parents who felt that fairy-tales glamorized cruelty and perpetuated prejudices. It was even thought likely that fairy-tales had created wicked stepmothers.

We were allowed to read *Peck's Bad Boy,* a book about an unspeakable brat who appealed to my brother Leon's imagination. Inspired by this book, we spread Limburger cheese on the chandelier, on the windows and on every contact point in the dining room.

Grandpa, uninhibited and robust, was no censor. He introduced me to the theatre because he liked it and, as it proved, so did I. Proctor's Theatre Stock Company at 58th Street and Third Avenue played terrifying melodramas like *The Still Alarm* and *The Ninety and Nine.* As the hero's head neared the sawmill wheel, or as the train puffed toward the heroine tied to the tracks, I shivered so vigorously that the row of seats trembled. *Shenandoah,* a violent pageant to which my mother took me, featured noise, smoke, cannon and soldiers falling to the ground and spurting tomato-juice blood. Fortunately I did not see enough of these cruel performances to make me as callous as the children who watch television today.

Pop's censorship of our reading matter started too late to be effective and lasted right through my college years. It was spotty, too, and functioned only when books like Upton Sinclair's *The Jungle* and Elinor Glyn's *Three Weeks* were forced on his attention. He had no idea that at the same time I was studying Restoration drama with the brilliant teacher, Algernon Tassin. My sister and I were forbidden to read certain stories in the newspaper, such as the account of the Thaw murder trial, up to the day I became a reporter.

At first Eddie and I thought it might be a good idea to censor our children's reading matter. When Dorie was five years old she taught herself to read because I refused to read comics to her. At that point we abandoned censorship. Any book in the house was theirs for the picking up. If anything was beyond their understanding, it could do no harm. It would merely bore them. They picked up strange things occasionally, to be sure. When Dorie was eight years old, she listened to "Information, Please" and answered a question that stumped the experts: "What woman annoyed her husband by eating too many sweets?" Dorie answered, "That's Nora in *The Doll's House.*" I was startled and asked, "How do you know?" She said, "Oh, I read it, you know, in the little red book." Why shouldn't a little child read a little red book called *The Doll's House*?

Later we had to choose between preventing them from listening to the radio and setting them apart from their friends. But we needn't have bothered. After a while Dorie said, "I don't like Superman any more. He's too super." They sang commercials at first with great glee and, when they had colds, wept happily over soap operas. Television, too, wore out its threat. They soon tired of it, maintaining unanimity with their group.

Eddie was a first-rate antidote to mass-production amusement. Every night he told the children tall tales about Captain Merriwell. He sang "The Elephant Sat on the Railroad Track" and recited Daniel Webster's most florid speeches at bedtime. I had to make up stories for them because it was easier than remembering.

While he asserted himself constantly in favor of rationality and fun, Eddie allowed himself to be excluded from problems like feeding and measles, and he quailed at the slightest sign of his children's disapproval.

A father's fear of asserting himself as a parent sometimes seems pathological. At a public swimming pool a three-year-old boy hurled himself to the ground next to his father and asked, "Daddy, can I go in now?" The father looked around, bit his upper lip, and answered, "Go ask your mother." The boy whined a little. "I can't find her." The man was really perplexed. He stood up and looked around and then drew himself up proudly; he had found the right answer. "If I see her, I'll certainly give her your message."

"What a dope," said my ten-year-old daughter. "He should have said yes. It's nice and warm."

Historically, I suppose there is some truth in the theory that women have shut men out of the nursery because men rule everywhere else and women want the nursery for their own domain.

For the past few decades women have been accused of usurping the authority of the male. Chief among our accusers is the creator of that eagerly accepted epithet, "Momism," Philip Wylie, whom I remember as a brilliant and charming young writer in our office. He may, I think, be wrong. Isn't it possible that Mother is so often Mom because Father refuses to be Pop? Fortunately our new generation of young fathers has decided to take an active part in bringing up the children and rounding out the family picture.

At one point I decided, to Eddie's bewilderment, that our well-adjusted children should receive the most modern and scientific care possible. At this misguided period I engaged a psychology major at Teachers' College as nurse and explained to her that she was to walk them in the park and give them the type of intelligent care that she would give neurotic children although, I stressed, these children were completely normal. After a week she came to me trembling with anger and frustration. "Your children are normal," she accused. "What do you want me for?" It was clearly a mistake to impose an abnormal nurse on normal children.

Although I was right to study what child psychologists wrote, I should have realized then as I do now that much of what they offered was tentative and perishable. I would have been happier if child psychologists had talked softly and if they had warned me not to believe them too wholeheartedly.

My daughters think now that they suffered from my psychological approach: "We never knew whether you were praising us because you meant it or because you were trying to build up our ego." There is nothing intrinsically wrong with trying to build up a child's ego, but we simply did not have enough knowledge of how to build a healthy personality.

If my generation failed to improve the human race, it was not because we read and thought too much, but because too little was known about how to transmogrify a child into a mature and worthy adult.

Suddenly, when you feel that only luck made your children turn out so well, they reward you unexpectedly. Dorie at twenty-five said she had tried to persuade a friend to visit the Charleston Gardens. She explained why. "I was only ten years old when you took Anne and me there. We just walked and walked through azaleas all day long for days, and rode in little boats in the cypress gardens. I'll never forget it. It was wonderful."

Before Dorie was born I enrolled in a course for expectant mothers at Teachers' College, hoping to learn something of value, but the second lecture was devoted to a description of a lethal abnormality so rare that it would have been better not to mention it at all in this short course.

My mother-in-law was politely surprised when she saw my vacation reading for a two weeks' stay at Atlantic City before my first daughter was born—half a dozen books on prenatal and infant care. She flicked them with a finger and said, "I had six children without books."

After reading all sorts of books on child care by all sorts of people, I became skeptical. They seemed so dogmatic, so rash. Doctors who would not think of prescribing ipecac generally for a million babies' stomach aches seemed to think it was all right to prescribe psychic treatment for the babies of a million readers. It is easier to buy advice on behavior than to buy a pill. You merely lift a few words from a page. Too often writers about children have not tried out their ideas clinically, but they do not hesitate to dispense them widely and irresponsibly. The results can be deadly.

We parents need experts. We need specific advice on the great problems we face day after day. What we get is a constantly changing mass of untested theory. So-called experts harry and confuse us with bits of ideas.

We need no book burnings, but we do need better and more science. We need to be reminded that no one yet has the final answer, that we are all groping for the truth.

CHAPTER FIVE

Horse and Buggy Layman

"For a consumption, an approved receipt by a lady of Paddington . . . the yolk of a new laid egg, some rose water . . . new milk from the cow . . . sirop de capillaire . . . nutmeg."

"Mr. Powel . . . was in so deep a decline as to be scarce able to walk; . . . and he was given over by his physician . . . He happily went to lodge at Paddington; the woman of the house understanding his condition, recollected that an old lady who had lodged in the same house, had left a book with a collection of receipts in it for various disorders, instantly fetched it and found the foregoing which he, having strictly followed, found himself much better in a fortnight . . . with the blessing of God, in a short time by degrees he recovered his health to the astonishment and surprise of all . . . and did not scruple to tell several persons the means and method of his recovery. N.B. This receipt I had from his own mouth."

"By a Lady" in MDCCLXXVIII

Fifty million women ought to be imprisoned for practicing medicine without a license. For diagnosing, prescribing, dosing and indulging in surgery as I have done for thirty-three years. No one has complained of my mistakes or even questioned my right to malpractice. On the contrary, it is taken for granted that I am equipped by sex with medical skill and wisdom.

Men are naïve in many ways about women, but they stake too much on the wisdom of ministering angels.

The practicing of lay medicine was forced on me when Eddie came down with pneumonia one month after we were married. Although I was as ignorant as a savage, the caduceus of Aesculapius was pinned on my shoulder. It was clear that my new husband had complete faith in my ability to take care of him. I was expected to know what to do for hives, a toothache, a sore throat, a sty on the eyelid.

Eddie's pneumonia was a terrifying initiation into my new job as amateur medical chief. I would have been less frightened if Eddie's family doctor had been, in fact, a tribal medicine man. As it was, I knew no science, and had no faith in myths, incantations or old wives' tales. I had nothing to guide me but emotions and a few strange memories of parental attitudes. Mother used to tell me, "Pop wouldn't allow the doctor to use icepacks when Bea had diphtheria."

"Keep the windows open," ordered Eddie's doctor, and a blast of freezing wind roared into our bedroom in Washington Mews.

"Won't he catch cold?" I asked, wondering if a pneumonia victim could catch further cold.

"Oh, no," beamed the doctor. "You should see our treatment of pneumonia at the hospital. Patients are put on a terrace and covered with sheets which we spray with ice water. If he isn't better tomorrow we'll give him antibodies," and he left us.

"What's antibodies?" I asked the nurse as we closed the windows. "I think it's stupid to freeze a person who has a cold."

The nurse explained grimly, "They give them these antibodies, and when the fever goes up to 107 and the bed begins to dance, the doctors go away."

I decided against antibodies and cold fresh air and the nurse slid a hot-water bottle against Eddie's feet. "Warm now?" she asked.

It takes a good deal of tact for a layman to differ with her doctor and not injure the physician-patient relationship. In that early test case I merely neglected to inform the doctor that I was going to pit my ignorance against his skill and experience. I had a vague feeling that I ought to have known something about pneumonia, and perhaps I had a premonition of other times, other illnesses, other doctors.

I was lucky, not wise or scientific in my negativism. I have never solved the problem of how to disagree with a scientist who knows his field, when I am aware of my own lack of knowledge. Occasionally, however, I have done it, with Eddie's backing. Although I knew nothing about medicine except that young doctors were socially charming, played tennis badly and liked good music, nothing in my background justified my husband's faith in my medical effectiveness.

It was fairly simple to be family medicine woman when I was a child at the beginning of this slightly hypochondriac century. My mother gave us castor oil when we ate too much and cod-liver oil when we ate too little. When we were too thin we got iron or malt syrup, viscous and sweetish brown, that flowed slowly from a bottle. For head colds we were given an extra handkerchief to take to school. Rashes were soothed with zinc salve. As far as anyone knew, we had no allergies, I.Q.'s or sibling involvements. Dr. Henry Herman came panting upstairs to treat complaints such as measles and whooping cough, and his fine deep voice, pleasant, warm manner and heavy gold watch that chimed the time, inspired us with complete confidence.

"Stick out your tongue. Hmm—nice and red." Putting his ear to our backs, he muttered, "Say ninety-nine." Pulling down an eyelid, he announced, "A trifle anemic."

Mother was a conscientious nurse, but she was too sympathetic. A skinned knee must have been very painful to her because she scolded us wrathfully, "You naughty child, how could you be so stupid? Why don't you look where you are going?" To this day I have a sense of guilt about illness and hide it until it becomes obvious to everyone. "For goodness' sake, why are you limping that way?"

As a child of eight my mother had helped take care of her eleven-months-old baby brother. "He had pneumonia and diphtheritic croup," she recalled. "My fingers were blistered from wringing out icepacks day and night. I loved my baby brother so," she continued, "and I was all alone with him when he died. I remember I fainted afterwards. When I came to, I heard the organ grinder playing, 'Cradle is empty, baby is gone . . .' He played that song and I cried."

My own medical experience was limited to an incident at a summer hotel in Long Island, when a flurry of nurses gathered and shrieked around a little girl whose face grew black. Her eyes bulged and her finger was in her mouth. According to fairy-tales, my only scientific literature at the time, that meant something was stuck in her throat.

"Turn her upside down and hit her back," I told the nurses. They swung her up by her heels, pounded her and out popped a small green apple.

Eddie teased me that this childhood episode is an example of feminine intuition functioning precociously but properly to conserve human life. I do not believe in intuition, medical or female; I believe in intelligence applied to a total of collected experience.

I had neither experience nor knowledge of other people's experience when I took on my new job of health expert for my new family. I learned quite soon that my chief responsibility was to diagnose symptoms. I had thought diagnosis was the function of doctors. However, doctors must wait to make a diagnosis until women decide whether or not a condition justifies consulting a doctor.

We visited friends one evening and were ushered into the bathroom, where the wife was patting the back of her husband's neck with Listerine. "It's a bad carbuncle," she explained in a professionally optimistic voice. Her husband said, beaming, "Isn't she wonderful? She's better than any doctor." She really wasn't, as he probably realized several operations later. He put too great faith in her intuitive knowledge. Her mistake was not to recognize that his neck was in danger.

Deciding whether or not professional advice is necessary is confusing and difficult. Do you telephone the doctor about a sore throat and 100° temperature at three o'clock in the afternoon, or do you gamble that it won't go up to 105° at midnight? Doctors are busy during the day and need to sleep at night. You are expected to guess correctly. You must, by some mystic formula, weigh the urgency of a writhing pain against your conviction that doctors are entitled to free holidays.

Christmas, Easter and the Fourth of July always present special problems. Your child is suffering. You pace the room and stub your toe on the dilemma—will the doctor think you a nuisance if you telephone him, or think you stupid if you don't? On a blizzardy Christmas Day I wondered why Doris seemed so ill. Her sore throat and low fever did not, I thought, justify her great prostration. Dr. Jerome Kohn listened to a description of her condition, and left his plum pudding. "Good you called me," he said after his examination. "She has infectious mononucleosis. I don't like plum pudding anyway." He patted my shoulder and went out into the snow.

I guessed wrong on a summer day, and the doctor rode out to Port Chester to make sure that Dorie had an upset stomach, not appendicitis. How was I to know the difference? I made the wrong decision when a bad pain kept me awake all night. I refused to call the doctor. In the morning he was politely annoyed.

"You know I wanted to see that pain in action. Why didn't you phone me?"

"At three o'clock?"

"Certainly. I stayed awake until five waiting for your call."

Even splinters are moot. Do they require professional skill or is my flame-sterilized needle adequate? The last splinter I tried to remove had branches and roots spread all through Anne's heel. I worked at it for a while and taxied her to Dr. Kohn, not at all prepared for his scolding. "Don't you know better than to lacerate a foot like that? Never touch a mushy splinter."

Anne sat on her next splinter and, remembering his scolding, I took her at once to Jerome. "That's a job for a surgeon," and we went around the corner. The surgeon raised his eyebrows in pleasure and went to work with cocaine, scalpel and tiny forceps. The splinter came out with a ping. Anne slid smiling from the operating table and asked wistfully, "What'll I tell the girls at school?"

I knew that some things are ignominious and some are noble. I brought up a full battery of semantics. "Tell them that a deep incision was made under local anesthetic," and here the surgeon filled in gravely, "and an inch-long hardwood splinter was excised." He helped her memorize it.

Even a pimple may require preliminary diagnosis. "You will think I'm crazy," I apologized to Jerome, "but Dorie has a tiny pimple on her face. It's no bigger than a pinhead, and it's white and shiny. I've never seen one like it." To my astonishment he asked to see it and congratulated me on having called him. "It's impetigo, and you caught it before it spread."

I failed to see a physician when Anne's finger had a small cut. I applied wet dressings for three days and, alarmed by her finger's strange color, finally consulted a doctor. He was angry when he looked at it. "Keep that wet dressing off. Don't you know better than that? It's all macerated." I consulted my dictionary. Macerated, I found, means "to reduce to a soft mass by soaking."

You diagnose a speck in someone's eye as unimportant, only to find that it is a steel splinter that an ophthalmologist must cut from the cornea. The next speck in someone's eye you are afraid to handle. You take your child to the same oculist, who touches her eyeball lightly, looks at you contemptuously, and presents a bill for five dollars.

Your daughter turns her ankle painfully, and you wait a day for the pain to disappear. The ankle, says the doctor, is badly sprained. "Why didn't you bring her right away?" Your other daughter hurts her wrist. You take her at once to the orthopedist who says patiently, "A slight strain, I can't charge you for this visit."

Guessing that a condition needs a doctor doesn't always end one's responsibility. The doctor on occasion needs a clear report of symptoms and factors leading up to the illness. This demands intelligence, objectivity and a great deal of experience, if it is to be done right. Doctors necessarily assume that the housewife is medically ignorant, but quite illogically, it seems to me, they expect her to be a clear, knowledgeable and succinct reporter. If you leave out a few essentials, or stress a few coincidentals, you may be helping your doctor make a quick diagnosis that you both will regret.

It would be nice for doctors to have some foolproof method of extracting essential information, whether the patient or the mother is overimaginative, hypochondriac, stoic, inarticulate, or just plain stupid and forgetful. But even if they had time to list every possible symptom they would complicate the issue, because mothers, like internes and student nurses, are suggestible and likely to find any morbid condition they watch for.

Doctors are busy and may not take time to ask all the important questions. The hardest task of the amateur is to decide at what point she had better not have complete faith in the expert. With some tact she can induce him to call in a consultant. It took ten years of sacroiliac pain for me to decide that my doctor might not know the last word in treatment. Diathermy and bed rest had failed. I asked tentatively for an orthopedist and was sent at once to Dr. Robert Lippmann, who worked magic with exercise, a bed board and a girdle.

When Anne grew ill at an isolated village set above the sand dunes of Cape Cod, I lost faith in a doctor after the first three minutes. The courtly physician leaned over the child's bed and pulled up her foot.

"Have you ever had cerebral meningitis?" he asked. Lifting her arms, "Have you ever had diphtheria?" Turning her head about as if it were a faucet, he asked, "Have you ever had poliomyelitis—infantile paralysis?" Pushing her stomach, "Typhoid? Malaria?" I grimaced at Anne over his shoulder, as she giggled answers to the incredible inquisition.

"I guess she'll be all right. Give her these pills every hour, these every four hours, these every two." He poured a rainbow of pellets and capsules into five envelopes and wrote meticulously on each envelope. "What has she got?" I asked. He smiled benignly. "These will fix her up," he answered and departed.

Annie, aged ten, said as I poured the pills down the drain, "He didn't ask if I'd had leprosy, Mommy."

Next morning her temperature had dropped from 103° to 99° in the confusing way that fever usually behaves, but I wasn't encouraged. My skin still drifts from its moorings and I feel again the panic started by the doctor's cheery voice, "That's fine. Patient dismissed." I knew Anne was in for something serious. I had no faith in the pill doctor, but a telephone survey showed me he was a monopoly—except for Dr. Samuel Wolman of Johns Hopkins, who was there on a holiday. I clamored for him, and he came by late at night to see what the rumpus was about. Strangers, we eyed each other suspiciously, until he saw Anne's red cheeks and bright eyes.

"I'm on vacation, you know, and I have no license to practice in this state. I'm not even allowed to write a prescription."

"You're not going to leave me in the hands of that shotgun doctor?" I protested.

He explained gently. "You'll have to go on with him. But if it will comfort you, I'd like to drop in now and then to see how she is. Ask him to call me in as consultant."

The local doctor fought a cold war against the deal, but the consultation arrangement was consummated and Dr. Wolman, on a purely voluntary mission, dropped in five times a day for two weeks to see Anne through virus pneumonia. I can still see him poring over her chart at midnight, cajoling the other doctor in the early morning, discussing current topics and literature with me to stiffen my upper lip. He combined, in my eyes, all the virtues, morals, humanity and scientific skills of most people's ideal physician.

A hypochondriac friend of mine has worked out a system of controlled skepticism. She always doubles the doctor's orders. If one pill three times daily is good, two pills six times are better; she continues rest twenty days when he suggests ten. Her doctor halved his prescriptions. He was exasperated out of his ethics one day and said to me, "What's the matter with the woman? I told her to give her child a benzoin steaming. When I got there she had four of them going full blast. Wonder they didn't suffocate."

Occasionally it's a good idea to show complete disloyalty and transfer one's affections to a new doctor. This isn't easy because habits and allegiances are hard to break, because there is no way to find out how good your next choice may be, and because doctors disapprove of patients who shop around. It can be done, however, as I found when I abandoned my first baby's pediatrician, an impressively busy man who shrugged his shoulders and vanished in a hurry when I reeled off some puzzling symptoms. I went to work on the index of Holt's big *Diseases of Infancy and Childhood.* By triangulation I decided she was starting rickets. I was shocked, and changed to Dr. Jerome Kohn, my happiest medical decision. He found she did not have rickets, but was merely dressed too warmly. For eighteen lucky years he made all diagnoses and assumed all worries about my children's health up to the day they went to college. "That's when they graduate from a pediatrician," he explained. No more lollypops to sweeten an examination.

Only once or twice has my faith in doctors been slightly clouded and I have moved on to others. Once because of the delicate adjustment necessary to get thin. My physician was convinced that less and less food would make me better and better. Under his persuasive guidance I assumed the diet of a prisoner of war until I staggered around, a victim of beriberi and avitaminosis, but without losing one ounce.

My best friend's physician took me in hand. "You won't have any trouble at all. Take three grains of thyroid." They gave me jitters.

"Take phenobarbital—half a grain three times a day." That made me dizzy.

He nodded. "Take calomel," he ordered.

"Isn't that pretty poisonous?" I asked.

Again he nodded. "Take citrate of magnesia. It'll wash out the calomel."

What was I to think of that endless chain of cause and effect? I decided my friend's taste in doctors was queer.

Another doctor, whom someone swore by, sold me a highly promising scientific bill of goods: a three-day examination to discover the cause of a backache. The imposing first-class hospital that received me into one of its Procrustean beds turned rapidly into the cabinet of Doctor Caligari. Seated next to my bed, the busy doctor ripped the flap from an old envelope and worked out an agenda. I was able to hear his rapid mutters between loud-speaker summonses, "Dr. Christian wanted in the surgery—wanted in the emergency ward..."

"Now let's list the tests: blood, urine, skeletal x-ray," he improvised and then stuck. "Basal metabolism?" I offered. "Of course," he said and looked to me for further suggestions.

I learned that technicians and their instruments are fallible. The blood-tester struck oil and tried frantically to get a gusher of blood back into my arm. I watched him blow bubbles with the needle for awhile, fascinated at their size and number until, remembering some detective stories, I yelled: "Stop pumping air into my veins!" The basal metabolism machine broke down three times, a stomach tube collapsed—and so did I. A nurse woke me at five in the morning to see if I was asleep, another nurse, armed with grins and enema bags, gave me delusions of persecution.

The summing-up conference was by Dostoevski out of O. Henry. The doctor solemnly handed Eddie a paper strip marked with electrocardiograph squiggles and intoned, "You will see by this that she has a serious heart condition. She will have to give up all activities and . . ."

"Wait a minute, wait a minute," interrupted Eddie, holding up the chart. "This is Mr. Bolocca's, it isn't my wife's!" The doctor vanished in a puff of shame, with no mention of the arthritis that had brought me to him. We never heard from him again.

A few of my friends believe implicitly in any new doctor. They rush from chiropractor to herbalist to swami to milk farm and back to the doctor.

There is an excellent but dangerous expedient for the skeptical housewife who wants to check up on treatment. She can read medical literature. But it takes a lifetime of study to become a thoroughly ignorant layman. You read the *Journal* of the American Medical Association and irritate your doctor when you venture: "Won't this estrogen give me cancer?" (He knows all about it.) You read the science columns in newspapers, put your trust in Marguerite Clark's medical columns in *Newsweek*. You spend days at the library of the New York Academy of Medicine going through books and magazines that occasionally cancel each other out.

The year after the Chicago epidemic, a young doctor decided Eddie had amoebic dysentery. I didn't believe him because he was as excited and pleased as if he had discovered uranium in his front lawn. A day at the library convinced me the doctor knew nothing about the disease and that he hadn't made a valid test. I told Eddie he was suffering from a disaffinity with corn.

"What nonsense!" said a surgeon. "Laymen have no right to read medical literature. They can't understand the implications in the first place. Can't discriminate between exceptions and universals. Besides, they must be morbid or hypochondriacs. What have you learned with all your medical reading?"

"Enough to fill a short paragraph," I answered. "I can boil down all I know to a few effective rules. If you have a pain, take an aspirin."

"Wrong!" barked the surgeon. "Aspirin masks symptoms." But I have found that a great many symptoms get discouraged if you mask them, and go away.

If you believe in your doctor, and you should, let him do your worrying.

Never, never, never study your own symptoms.

If a condition is really serious, withdraw from the conference table and obey implicitly.

"Your rules are pretty good," admitted the surgeon, "but tell me, honestly, what you think you can get out of reading such stuff?"

"Doctors are all very well," I explained, "but they are too busy. I haven't a court physician. They don't take time to ask the right questions, they forget who you are and don't put the pieces together right. My cousin's doctor prescribed eggnogs and ice cream to build her up, and forgot she had a bad gall bladder. And they don't even answer questions. They're apt to be sliding into the driver's seat before you can ask: 'When do I stop this medicine? Should I call you if his fever goes up? Should I stop the aureomycin if it makes her sick?' "

"What else do you think a layman gets out of reading medical literature?" he asked.

I plunged. "Psychology and psychosomatics." The American Medical Association *Journal* is full of psychosomatics that is written for doctors but that could help laymen. A woman can't live unless she knows some psychology. Her role is family peacemaker.

Unfortunately, my young motherhood was bedeviled with psychology. We had to feel the pulse of every word and measure every act. We tried to prevent neuroses by handling children perfectly. We really thought wise parents could make the next generation normal.

We had to do so much understanding, so much building up of egos. Why is the child cross? Aha! Because the invitation to her friend's party hasn't arrived yet. Sherlock Holmes finds the crime and soothes the victim until the postman comes. One of the children snarls at Eddie? What's wrong? Heavy thought. He forget to kiss her when he came home.

Your child has been moody for three hours—a very long time. You get out a jigsaw puzzle and as you play, lead the conversation in every possible direction until suddenly you find the barb. "What's bad about a Jew? Nelly said I was a Jew." That is a fretful question for an amateur, even for a professional. But one answers as satisfactorily as one can. "There are good people and bad people in every country and religion. But little girls who are unkind aren't worth your thinking about."

Taking care of sick children calls for that ancient commodity, mother-wit, a semi-conscious pun on psychology. My mother-wit says, "Don't train a sick child, but do keep it happy." Comic books may be bad for well children, but they are good medicine for the sick. A quiet sick room is irritating and exhausting to a young patient with 103° fever. "Mommy, please leave the door open so I can hear what they are saying." A cheerful room might seem proper, but children convalesce on the sobbings of daytime serials. "It's fun, Mommy. Why don't you listen to it? Don't go."

But a normal attitude toward illness isn't always satisfactory to a child. Sometimes there is romance in sickness, which one can spotlight successfully. Exotic props and words work magic.

"Mommy, haven't I something more important than grippe? Please, Mommy."

"You have atypical pneumonia," I say, afraid she may be frightened.

Her languid eyes fly wide open. "Oh, how wonderful," she gurgles between coughs and sails right through the crisis.

You break the news, "Let's go to the dentist," and find the child is delighted. "When can I have a brace on my teeth? It's so noble!" Or you hope: "I think your ankle is sprained," only to hear, "I hope not. I hope it's broken. Then I can have a crutch."

Coping with your children's shyness, your friends' inferiority complexes, your own masochism is quite different from being drawn into psychopathology, the most annoying branch of a housewife's medical practice. Although my ignorance is profound, people ask me, and everyone else presumably, questions that would embarrass William Menninger. The shyest man I know asked if he should be psychoanalyzed, but I had no opinion. He did, and now he no longer walks into a room like a half-cooked crab.

We read a few books, but never the one that is needed in an emergency. A few years ago I thought my maid had intestinal flu, but the doctor disagreed. "You have a psychiatric case on your hands," he said bluntly. "She thinks *'they'* poisoned her. Did you know she thinks her last employers tried for a whole month to murder her on their yacht off the coast of Florida?"

"That's a long time to not-succeed in killing someone," I said. "Paranoia?"

"Advanced," he said.

My ignorance endangered my family once when I almost failed to see that our superb cook's super-temperament had crossed the border. She was writing her autobiography, as all women seem to do, happily when it went well, and furiously when the butcher's boy wouldn't listen to it. Suddenly something seemed vaguely disturbing. I telephoned the doctor, "Her manic-depressive periods used to change every few months, but now they seem to change every day or so. What should I do?"

"Is she ever violent?" he asked. I passed the question to the waitress, who rolled her eyes. "Sure, she throws pots and knives around and chases us out of the kitchen." Why hadn't I found out about that sooner?

"Get her out at once. Get her out at once," came the doctor's voice in an urgent sing-song.

A surgeon who was listening to a discussion on amateur psychiatry said, "Normal laymen can't understand psychiatry and morbid ones shouldn't try. Why do you read about it?"

"Trends," I answered.

"Oh, trends, that's different. You have to know trends as a public relations counsel." Then, as an afterthought, "What trends?"

"For one thing it's interesting to see that we're going back to placebos." People used to cure warts by burying frogs at midnight. Samuel Peck applies a placebo directly to the wart. It cured my daughter even though she knew it was a placebo. Prayers, witch doctoring still work magic. Once a sedative failed to relieve a back pain in two hours. A doctor, judging wisely that a delayed reaction was starting in, pricked my arm with a hypodermic needle, pretending to inject demerol. I knew this was just the old placebo technique, but I was fascinated to find that knowing about it did not interfere at all with the course of the prior dose.

"That may be true," interrupted an anthropologist, "nevertheless doctors hate knowledgeable patients. The old tradition—mystery."

"Nonsense," exploded the surgeon. "If we took time out to explain etiology, treatment, prognosis—my lord, think of the time it would take to argue points."

A general practitioner on the other hand, said, "It is helpful to have informed patients. They often help you to make a proper diagnosis."

He, I am afraid, was being polite. My knowledge doesn't even include ordinary nursing skills. Bandaging, for example. Gauze for Anne's sore finger went as far as the wrist, and on one extravagant occasion went around her forearm, her elbow and her shoulder until it ended in a fine bow at the neck. Johnson and Johnson should welcome such inefficiency.

Obviously the fumbling layman is not the answer to the serious problem of patient-physician relationship. Unless there is mutual understanding and communication both patient and physician are at an enormous disadvantage. Fifty years ago there was a little science and a great deal of friendship in doctoring. Today science is overwhelmingly complex, and the doctor is rarely an old friend. Who can open a communications channel quickly between a physician and patient who wonders what sort of man he is facing? How can the two get together medically even on objective symptoms? Today the good physician, like Dana Atchley and Hamilton Southworth, must try to gauge personality imponderables, such as tension, before prescribing treatment or medication.

A young mother of three children complained, "If only someone would give me a clue to what my doctor thinks. He rakes me with an eye as cold as a scalpel and says, 'I'd go to bed if I were you.' What does he mean by that? Is he calling me a milksop, or is he warning me that I'll die if I don't go to bed?"

"What do you suggest—a personality profile of your physician?" asked an internist.

A delightful idea. Every doctor should give his patient a personality chart.

Dr. ℞ is: (check correct classification)

An Alarmist—You are not as sick as he thinks.

An Appeaser—You are sicker than he says.

A Straddler—He can't make up his mind. Figure it out for yourself.

A Cynic—Thinks Nature is the best doctor; all medicine is dangerous or useless.

A Genius—Knows what's wrong by inspiration.

An Absent-minded Scientist—He forgets pieces of the puzzle. Keep him posted as to blood pressure, kidney stones.

A Gadgeteer—You are in for lots of tests, but he may not use all the results.

A Doctor—Knows all, puts it together and tells you all you should know.

And, to help the doctor, there should be a personality chart of the patient.

Jones is: (check correct classification)

A Hypochondriac—It is painful but advisable to listen to his symptoms; he may be telling the truth.

A Stoic—Hides or minimizes symptoms. Give him the third-degree.

A Realist—Likes the truth.

A Romantic—Wants only pleasant truths.

A Pessimist—Believes only unpleasant news.

The Immature (nearly everybody)—should be:

Bullied
Charmed
Babied

"Nonsense!" said the internist. "The doctor is supposed to know his patient."

The trouble is the doctor hasn't time to study his patient.

I don't know how to choose a doctor. My best friend took the advice of the doorman at his apartment house, and thinks the choice was lucky. Another friend called the local hospital, looked up the wrong name in the telephone book and was attended presently by a man who had just been deprived of his license to practice.

I don't know whether or not to call in a doctor for an acute symptom, or a tedious chronic condition, or a vague malaise. When Eddie asks, "Do you think the pain in my back is my kidneys?" I oughtn't to be allowed to answer, as I do, "Let's see how it feels tomorrow."

I don't know what questions to ask the doctor. Often I cannot remember what he told me to do. I don't know why women should be expected to start in before the scientist comes and continue, without training, where he leaves off. I am unfettered intuition. I am the tribal medicine woman. Mankind has nevertheless survived in spite of eons of error.

I know only that the amateur way to health is neither straight nor safe.

CHAPTER SIX

Miles of Aisles

A woman is always buying something.

OVID: *Ars amatoria,* I, c. 2 B.C.

"When Lincoln was assassinated," said my mother, "Grandpa used up every inch of black goods to drape his store inside and out. And in front he hung a large oval placard painted with the words, 'Mourn, Ye People, Mourn' . . . That was the year I was born."

Grandpa's Fancy and Dry Goods Store on Avenue D near Fourth Street was one of the earliest one-price stores in the city. One-price meant that goods were quoted at a firm figure, and customers took them or left them and no argument. As a child Moth measured and wrapped and learned arithmetic by doing. She also learned through selling how to buy. She understood as I never have the magic process which transmutes effort into money, money into purchases and purchases into use.

I learned a little about shopping as a child of six, in 1898, when I dragged my high-buttoned shoes behind her long dress as it swept the dusty aisles of Altman's, Stern's and McCreery's. While I tried to keep out of the way of advancing ladies, Moth halted at every counter to concentrate on the displays.

One day I stopped watching the wire baskets flying on shining wires under the ceiling when I caught sight of the pins strewn on the rough wooden floor at the ribbon counter. Children at that time were slaves to rhymes.

"See a pin and let it lay,
You'll have bad luck all the day.
See a pin and pick it up,
All the day you'll have good luck."

I harvested pins from the floor until my coat glistened from collar to hem, and looking up, found myself surrounded by a circle of laughing women. I wanted to cry because I felt they were unkind and rude. I still feel that I am likely to be uncomfortable in department stores.

Nobody, but nobody, can convince me that department stores are designed for the pleasure, convenience or health of the public. These monstrous obstacle courses wear out the customers. My limit of endurance is under an hour. After that I want to lie down in a cozy aisle and go to sleep.

"Mommy, will you go with me for a coat?" asked Annie, and, as I consented, I thought unhappily of the miles and miles of aisles I would have to walk, burdened by my own heavy coat that couldn't be checked anywhere. We walked half a block to the elevators and asked the starter what floor we should try. He looked Annie over with a pleased smile and suggested, "Try the third. And you might go to the second. If they haven't it, go to the fourth. And the budget shop is on the seventh. Going up." My numbers may not be accurate or my titles correct, but we rode up and down and walked back and forth through Junior Misses, Youngs, Sports, Debutantes, Teens and the like until our mileage was greater than our desire for a coat, and we went home.

Road maps and guides in these stores are not completely helpful. "Oh, no, blankets aren't on this floor. Try the third floor rear." A half a block to the escalator and down one side, around the corner and down another, and another half block to the rear.

I took a young bride shopping for dining room equipment. Silverware on the main floor, china on the fourth, linens on the third, a lazy susan in the fifth-floor gift shop and candles in the basement. Our feet grew heavy as we walked and stood. I have special shoes, built for standing in. They are not as pretty as a traffic cop's, but I don't use them as frequently.

"Things are too scattered," said a woman who shops for all her busy family. "A girl will show you a display of silverware and you say 'Is that all there is?' and she says, 'I think there are some over there in that section.' "

Shopping is like blind-man's buff or hide-and-seek. You blunder around for merchandise, while the selling force skips about nimbly in evasion movements. The object of the game is to capture the goods against overwhelming efforts to defeat you.

In the nineteenth century variety shops were small, customers few, and salespeople plentiful. Grandpa's Fancy and Dry Goods Store must have been delightful for his customers in 1865. He knew them all by name, teased and scolded them when they were difficult. But they were all his friends and neighbors.

One day Moth heard a woman complain, "This poplin is too narrow."

Grandpa lifted the bolt high in the air, said, "But look, see long long it is," and dropped it on her fingers. She probably forgave him. When I knew him years later, he was still charming and handsome with a cute puckish face, smiling blue eyes, and a smart gray goatee.

His sales force of twenty-five men and women worked hard and obsequiously. They earned five dollars a week and worked from 8:00 A.M. to 9:00 P.M. on weekdays, and until midnight on Saturdays. Bachelors slept on hard wooden counters at night, under darkened gas lamps. This method of augmenting wages was not unusual. Some larger stores maintained severely regulated dormitories for their clerks.

"But Grandpa was a pioneer in labor relations," Moth told me. "Some people thought he was quite a radical. When he sold out his store after a few years and built his cigar factory at 71st Street and York Avenue, he bought all the tenements around it to rent to his workers. People were sure he was going too far when he turned the factory yard into a playground."

Labor conditions have improved since then, but relations between seller and buyer have deteriorated. At the beginning of our century, stores still catered graciously and individually to wealthy ladies. Today, however, this ancient individual method has no validity for the thousands of customers that throng a department store in a single day. There seems to be a gap between mass production and unit purchasing. I feel sorry for stores, in a way. How can they turn a horde of individuals into a like-minded buying unit? I asked Tobé, the famous merchandise consultant, and co-director of the Tobé-Coburn School, what the greatest problem of department stores is. She answered quickly. "The point of sale." That is my great problem, the point of purchase. A long chain of impulses—advertisements, TV or radio commercials and catalogues have brought me into the store. But the weakest link is the actual transaction. As far as I am concerned the chain breaks right there. I decide that I don't need anything anyway and go home, empty-handed.

One Christmas season Eddie and I walked through Bloomingdale's main floor. We counted eighteen customers at the handbag counter and one salesperson to take care of them.

Eddie figured that if this one salesclerk were to give five minutes to each customer—a low estimate considering the heaped-up confusion of the counter—the last person would wait one hour and twenty-five minutes to be waited on—if he waited. Department stores are short on arithmetical imagination. They fail to add up and multiply the number of sales that cannot be consummated, on a time-service basis.

I went to Macy's to buy a complete painting outfit for Aunt Rose, hoping that she would begin painting again after thirty years devoted to housework. I expected also to buy a set of china, eight yards of blue corduroy, half a dozen books and several other items. I stood in each department for about five minutes at the edge of waiting crowds. I left without buying anything. Unless other consumers melted away in discouragement as I did, my waiting period would have been very roughly three days.

I took my daughters to Bonwit Teller's fancifully decorated specialty shop to buy their spring clothes. The dress department had only a pair of customers, one saleswoman and a section manager walking about with firm, executive tread. We waited for recognition. After a few minutes we asked for help. "You have to wait your turn," she said severely. "No, indeed I don't," I answered, and we went across the street to Rosette Pennington's pleasant shop, where Dorie and Anne bought their wardrobes in an hour, while I drank coffee, served in a spirit of promotional wisdom.

When I was young and insecure I was a timid and worried customer, but I did my best to be poised, gracious and patient in a store because my mother did so well on the principle of courtesy. I learned that the usual salesclerk has too many duties in connection with each sale. She must (collectively) pull heavy bolts of material from shelves, run around to fitting rooms to pick up the dresses she knows aren't on the racks, call up the stock room to replenish her stock, answer the phone on an inquiry, write out sales slips, open countless drawers to find the right sized nightgowns, hurry the wrapping clerk, yell for the section manager. If I were a salesclerk in a department store I should go mad.

"Who does she think she is to call me Miss?"

Clerks do not want to annoy their customers, even if some act as if that were their goal. But I am amazed at their "mystic systems," as one clerk called it, for sizing up their customers. I listened to a business transaction at Lord & Taylor one day.

"Watch this," my salesman said to me, and winked.

"Can I help you, Madam?" he asked a short heavy woman who was tugging at a length of rayon in a snarled pile.

She smiled gratefully and said, "Oh, yes. Do you have this in yellow?"

"Sorry, Madam, we don't," he answered. He pivoted around to me and pointed his thumb at a pile of yellow rayon on another table. I was astounded.

"Why did you tell her you had none?" I asked.

"She didn't want to buy, she's just a shopper. You can tell in a minute by the way they come up to you."

On another day, in another store, I watched a tight-lipped clerk add up a long sales slip. When the customer left she slammed her salesbook closed and glared. "She'll return 'em all. I gotta mind not to send 'em to her at all."

Salespeople's attitudes toward customers' spending are pointers in the economic wind. I can remember when no one dared to say to a salesperson, "That is too expensive." In a more extravagant era it was not surprising to hear a salesman at Tiffany's apologize to a customer, "I'm very sorry, Madam, we're fresh out of gold lipsticks."

Now, however, the salesperson is part of the purchasing public herself. She identifies herself with the customer, disapproves of the extravagant woman and cooperates, if she has time, with the careful buyer. At Bergdorf Goodman's a pretty red-haired girl tucked a handbag back on the shelf and smiled at me. "I don't blame you a bit. Forty dollars is too much for that bag." She leaned across the counter confidentially and said, "A woman just bought three for seventy-five dollars apiece. What do I care how they spend their money?"

A few saleswomen have been my friends for years. We have lunch together after we have finished our chore. They tell me what retailing looks like from their side of the sales slip.

One friend of long standing complains to me, "I'm a fool. I practically never get out to lunch. If my customer comes in, how can I walk out on her?" She is like many devoted souls who gripe, but love their jobs and their store.

I admit that I have been guilty of returning goods I should not have bought. But I have been unable to resist the plea in the eyes of the salesclerk. I can't seem to say, "No, thank you," and walk out. I am impelled to say, "Thank you ever so much. Please send it to me." I should, of course, be penalized for this.

I have learned not to make salespeople my shopping scapegoats. They are symptoms of an aging institution.

Look at sizes! There is a fantastic lack of standardization in sizes of wearing apparel for women and children, although men's wear is more intelligently merchandised. When my husband asks for a size forty suit he knows that a forty-two will be larger and a thirty-eight smaller in any store.

When I started shopping for my first baby I learned that manufacturers marked sizes on a psychological basis. Mothers like to think their babies are big for their age, so it is flattering to buy a play suit marked size two for an eight-months baby. Every manufacturer has his own notion about how large the flattery should be.

How can you tell what size you're buying in children's clothes? Sock sizes seem to have been worked out by numerologists. Buying underpanties can't be done by size designation; one has to take along either measurements or samples.

The same eccentric lack of system applies to female clothing for all ages. You capture the attention of a shy wood nymph hiding behind clothes trees.

"What size, madam?"

"Size sixteen, please."

Her free-swinging high heels clop through the enticing door of the stockroom. She comes out after a few moments, tired and hot, her chin resting on an armful of dresses.

"This is size fourteen, but it's plenty large enough."

In the coat department the clerk shakes her head, "No, no,

you don't want sixteen. Our size twelve will fit you." It does.

Sizing of women's clothing is unfunctional. If you are tall you buy a woman's size whether you are a high-school girl or a grandmother. If you are fat you buy an old lady's dress. If you are small and slender you buy a misses' size in a style that may go ill with your silvery hair.

"Why don't they make more dresses for the average woman?" I asked. "The average woman, the United States government says, is about five feet three inches tall."

The saleswoman shrugged, "We tried to stock them but they sold so fast the manufacturer gave up making them."

At another store I was further instructed by an unhappy saleswoman who couldn't find a size sixteen, "Hundreds of women go away every day without buying because we have hardly any large sizes. You know, sizes over twelve."

"If they have so many customers for large sizes, why don't they stock them?" I asked.

"You know why manufacturers won't make large sizes?" she answered. "Designers are all fairies and they hate to look at heavy women so they refuse to make dresses for them." I didn't believe her facts and deplored her logic. There is comparatively little demand for large-size dresses, and manufacturers, I suppose, like volume sales best.

My daughter telephoned me from Cambridge last winter to ask cheerfully, "Where shall I buy a warm winter coat, Mommy?"

"You'll have to go around to all the shops," I said hopelessly.

She tried to get at it in another way. "What material should I buy that's warm?"

I couldn't give her specifications or descriptions because I didn't know any. There are too many variables.

I asked a famous designer, and she answered concisely, "Nobody knows what's in a material nowadays except experts."

A young woman, married a few months, fingered the hem of her skirt and asked, "How can you tell whether a material is good or not?"

"I have only one test for material," I told her. "I scrounge a piece together in my hand and if the wrinkles show, I don't buy it."

"That's right, you can tell by the feeling," said a woman who had matured through the process of shopping for four children.

I was confused. How can my fingers know more than my head? I protested, "Some fabrics feel fine and solid, but they have filler material or they are loaded. At the first cleaning the bottom drops out and you have very flimsy stuff left."

"What's loaded?" asked the bride. "What material is my dress made of?"

A textile manufacturer slid the hem between his thumb and forefinger. "I think—it feels like . . ." He lit a match and suggested hopefully, "I could tell by the way it burns."

She snatched away her dress and said, "I don't want to know that badly."

"If women don't even know what material they are buying, how can they tell whether it's any good for their purposes?" he asked insultingly.

On a number of occasions I have tried to find specifications for what I need. How does one buy a mattress for a sacroiliac sleeper? Orthopedists advise horsehair. I discovered there were many kinds of horsehair—tail, mane, curled, short, long and hog. After two weeks of intensive research I found out where the best manufacturer sold his mattresses at retail. When it was laid on my bed it seemed to be made of semi-solid concrete.

How does one appraise an overstuffed chair? You may look, feel, poke, push and, if there is no rope across the seat, even sit; but unless your store, like the Museum of Modern Art, shows you a cross-section, you are buying a mystery. The springs may sag, the legs may spring, or the chair may last until you die of boredom looking at it.

Should you buy this new kind of rug with glued back? Does it wear better than the old kind? I don't know.

Specifications probably would not help me decide on values. Moth used to say it's cheaper to buy the best. I can never decide if best means most expensive. Or if cheap things are expensive in the long run. How can one figure price against quality? How can one balance the values of utility and esthetics?

Should I try to be an expert on all products or should merchants and manufacturers be more helpful? I asked a friend whose home is perfectly equipped how she managed to pick out the right things. She protested, "You can't know the technicalities of everything. The thing to do is to trade at reputable stores and to take their word."

Experience is not an effective teacher. A well-run hotel knows how many years and how many washings to expect per sheet because it keeps records of quality and endurance. How long should my sheets last? A year? Two years? Five years? I don't know a thing about it. I ask the salesman, and whether he is knowledgeable or not, I take his advice. Bernice Fitz-Gibbon, appraising the problem of personalities, said to me, "Dale Carnegie has furthered the cause of charm and pretty smiles. But too often the technical training a salesperson should have is neglected while perhaps too much emphasis is put on smiling. A smile could never sell me a power mower or a vacuum cleaner."

Does this moisture-repellent raincoat shed water? No, it strains it. Is this heavy blanket warmer than the one weighing two pounds less? I'll never know because I do not buy both for testing purposes.

I watched a saleswoman pull out drawer after drawer of lovely blond wood and glass, searching for size six gloves. Some Kafka of retail merchandising must have developed the system of irrelativity. Arrangement décor has little connection with the convenience of the sales effort.

Lighting too often defeats its purpose. In a dress department you may look straight into an electric fixture, and you may find it impossible to dodge a shadow or hip-high gloom. A dress often hangs in its own eclipse. I have seen counter tops that mirror overhead lights and hide the powder compacts concealed below.

As it is, I enjoy buying in Lamston's or Woolworth's where everything is visible and clearly priced, where every item is within easy reach; where you don't even have to wait for service if you have enough small change in your purse.

I also enjoy buying things at Neiman-Marcus when Stanley takes Eddie and me around. Under the spell of his quiet hypnotic enthusiasm we order things we have wanted for years, or that we have never imagined we wanted.

We take it for granted, I am afraid, that the sales force is too small to sell us available merchandise. But why, I wonder, do stores too often advertise products they do not have? They spend a fortune to entice me into the retail parlor and at the point of sale throw away my interest.

When I read, "No phone or mail orders," I grow skeptical. Is the ad merely a sideshow spiel? Will the blankets be there to buy if I fight my way through traffic, or will the clerk say, "Sorry, we're all sold out"? I do not like to be lured to a shop to find that the bait is gone.

Sometimes the advertised article has never been stocked by the store. One day I went to a specialty shop that had illustrated a lovely silver bracelet in an expensive brochure gotten up just for me.

The saleslady listened carefully and said, "I don't know anything about it. Let me call the buyer." The buyer was worried at first, but her anxiety vanished as the situation became clear.

"We really have no bracelets like that; it's just an ad, you know."

A vendeuse blushed when I asked for the dress I had seen in *Vogue* that morning at the hairdresser's. "What's an ad got to do with merchandise? Did you see that black dress in our window? Four women have come in to buy it. Do we have it? No! It's a sample that we haven't got and can't get."

You telephone about bedspreads shown on page thirteen of a catalogue and win a frank admission over the wire, "It certainly is in the catalogue. But we've never had it, I know."

Advertising and merchandising departments occasionally seem to be on feuding terms. You write for an advertised carpet sweeper but two weeks later you receive a printed form betraying the quantitative nature of the rebuff. "The item you ordered is out of stock."

Because so many advertisements are not completely honest, I have a tempestuous resistance to all advertisements that deviate a hairsbreadth from exact factual descriptions. I can laugh at the contemptuous ads that give me nonsense instead of information, like an Altman ad that burbled: ". . . butcher rayon, fresh and spring-like as a dew-soaked meadow . . . and the meadow sprinkled lightly with flowers." I want no dew-soaked dresses. Certainly merchandising semantics needs a thorough going over.

Terms like pre-shrunk and rain-resistant are fighting words. Old-fashioned fireman-red nightshirts advertised in my morning paper seemed to be a perfect device for brightening the end of a day, so I ordered one for Eddie. It looked almost excessively gay on him. But the color ran when he dropped it onto a damp bath towel. We called up the store and the situation was clarified. "Oh, yes, the fireman-red nightshirts are guaranteed against running, but they will bleed in the first two or three washings."

Brooks Brothers, a store for men, advertised winter-weight tweed and cheviot overcoats admirably. "Brooks Brothers' overcoats have a double advantage . . . in addition to the fine 26- to 30-ounce overcoatings, we line some with 10½-ounce plaid woolens woven exclusively for us."

Russeks, a store for women, advertised overcoats less explicitly but more poetically: "Timeless wonder of warmth without weight or bulk . . . the classic coat that tops everything in buttersoft, Chinese cashmere." How can I possibly gauge the virtue of an overcoat described in luscious but faulty verse?

I have no systematic way to judge costs and values, but for a long while I aimed at perfection. Colors had to match, lines had to be right, material and workmanship good. But I have learned to be happy with a quick coincidence between what I need and what there is. At best I make an inglorious compromise between good taste and availability, between pleasure and common sense. Most of my friends take their job seriously and try hard to get the best value for their money.

Actually we are as diverse as our reasons for braving the rigors of department stores. Basically, we buy things we need. Secondarily, we buy things we want for esthetic or status values. Beyond that there are innumerable motivations that lead us to buy or that inhibit our purchasing.

It is not the sweet dream of all women to go window shopping on Fifth Avenue. Shopping is an extension of one's whole personality. It is mixed up with one's socio-political and economic views, and with one's philosophy, religion and patriotism.

My scale of spiritual values is as important as my money when I go shopping. In my purse are the things I learned at Sunday School and college, in my newspaper's woman's page, foreign reports and war news. When I stand at the counter trying to decide whether to take service weight or sheer nylons, these bits of knowledge and ideas rattle noisily to get my attention.

For one thing, my Puritanism stands ready to censor an extravagance. The Bible taught us that a camel had stuck in the eye of a needle and that nobility lies in self-deprivation. Whatever lessons we learn later about the status value of possessions, there remains a residue of this to complicate many a purchase. It's often a three-way battle—you, your conscience and the merchandise.

Basically, Eddie and I agree with Samuel Straus who wrote "Things Are in the Saddle" years ago in the *Atlantic Monthly*. Possessions complicate life. It is easy for me not to buy them.

Luckily, I have never had much time for shopping. Running a house, taking care of two children and working as a public relations counsel have seemed more important to me than acquiring things. It is amazing how even essentials can be done without. I spent one summer rejecting every item in a Sears, Roebuck catalogue. It was lots of fun.

When I think back on the thousands of packages that my tired hands have unwrapped, I am aghast that so few of them seem worth having today. Only a few are cherishable. A Duncan Ferguson cat, round, relaxed and brassy; a lovely satinwood desk bought at auction, too high and narrow to be practical; a Parker 51 pen that almost writes by itself; a Steinway piano which I rarely play, but that sings in mellow tones under Dorie's clever fingers; two dresses bought for my children at I. Magnin's in Los Angeles that were so lovely they refused to wear them; a dress Vionnet made for me during the flapper period that I am saving for the amazement of my future grandchildren. Nothing else? No. All other possessions were bought, used, but never loved.

Our lives are cluttered with things that have to be cleaned, repaired, protected, insured, watched over. A friend of mine was chained as miserably to her things as Andromeda to her rock. We spent the day at her home near London. "I'd love to go to the States to see my grandchildren," she wailed, "but

I can't." She pointed to her antique furniture. "I don't dare rent the house, the tenants might spoil them. And I can't leave it empty because the cold might spoil them."

Perhaps I am rationalizing my laziness. But I think I am not unique. Many of my friends agree that their attitude toward material things is the elastic band that keeps the roll of bills from opening too easily.

Many of us have learned to our surprise how easy and comfortable it is to scrap the notion that status depends on a shiny new surface. A shabby chair has become a symbol of good taste to many of us. "I used to think Boston women dressed ridiculously," said a successful advertising woman. "Sturdy, you know, but frumpy. But I've come around. They're right. Everything classic for me from now on. Never stylish, never out of style. Use it for years. Saves time, energy and money. And who cares anyway?"

It is hard for me to understand women who love shopping for its own sake. I cannot help feeling that they are neurotic. I recognize that I have often had irrational reasons for undergoing the masochistic ordeal of shopping. When everything was too much for me, when the locksmith didn't come, when work at the office piled up while I nursed Dorie through the grippe, when my back ached and the roof leaked, I seemed to think I could escape by pushing through crowds to buy sheets, uniforms, toys.

"I love shopping," a tense, well-dressed woman said to me. "I like it better than anything else in the world. When I feel terribly low, I call up my mother and say, 'Meet me for a little shopping.' We look at windows and go through stores all day. We go back to the same counter six times maybe to look again at a blouse and by evening we both feel much better."

What, I wondered, was she escaping? "I know how you feel," said a sad-eyed woman. "Whenever my husband has a hangover, I pound the aisles. It's the only thing that saves my reason." I turned to another woman, who had just boasted that she had spent the entire day looking for a belt. She blushed, because she realized that the perfect belt had no validity. She should have been painting, and her artistic energy had been short-circuited.

Sometimes I buy kitchen gadgets to cover up a deep feeling of dissatisfaction with clumsy kitchens. Gadgets that we know are impractical become lightning rods for our discontent.

"I buy every tricky thing on the market, to make things run smoothly," said a brisk young bride. Her friend, more experienced, sighed and said, "I gave away two barrels full of whirlers and twirlers and scrapers and shredders when I moved last month. They had all been used once."

A few women I know buy in a kind of gluttony to compensate for lack of love. But a glutton can never be satisfied. If there is not enough love to fill him, there is food, but never enough; there is drink, but never enough; there are sorrow or adulation or success or power or fame or punishment, but never enough. Of nothing is there ever enough for a glutton.

There are many kinds of gluttons in the world. But they have this in common—there is a leak in their ego.

One exquisite young woman buys continually because she is a narcissist. Clothes and household articles are projections of herself. Her body and her home must be adorned and admired. As she pirouetted in front of a mirror she said gaily, "I shop all day. I spend my time trying to make things look beautiful. I'm such a perfectionist."

More than once I have shopped to build up my ego. Letting Mr. John pick out a hat sets my adaptive syndrome to work.

A department store president said, "Occasionally you can do your ego a lot of good that way. But shopping never cured an inferiority complex. Women like that haunt the aisles of our store. Take women who have no careers. They feel very inferior. They don't think they're doing anything when they are 'just a housewife.' They have no personal status—only their husband's—and that isn't enough. They have to prove they are good at something, finding the best bargains, or the rarest things, or the showiest, or the most beautiful. When their husbands come home at night they can brag, 'See what I accomplished. I went to four stores and saved fifty cents on this egg-beater.' It satisfies their sense of rivalry too. They get a feeling of success."

As I look back over a lifetime of purchasing for my family, as I think of the weary miles of aisles I have walked in search of necessities, I try to look objectively at department stores, and come to the conclusion that there is generally a frivolous disregard for me as a customer because I am an amateur. My judgment is considered whimsical, my knowledge faulty and superficial, my time worth nothing and my legs tireless. They see me as an amateur, polite, patient and unprotesting most of the time. This attitude is a handicap to both sides of the sales counter.

"All women know how to shop." "Shopping is an instinct, a female characteristic." "Women have an innate sense of values." These easy definitions are a poor substitute for professionalism in purchasing.

I am a professional in my office, but when my foot haltingly crosses the threshold of a shop, I turn into an amateur. After thirty-three years as purchasing agent for my family I know as little about wares and values as I did when I watched Moth examine, appraise and reject a length of lace. I buy with an increasing lack of interest, skill and wisdom. It would be nice to be intelligent in this job, but I have not found a teacher, textbook or friend to help me find my way through the jungle. That is why I wear old dresses and sit on shabby chairs.

I like pretty clothes, good furniture, and other evidences of a pleasant sybaritic life. But my desire for these things isn't equal to the difficulty of acquiring them. Pushing through heavy revolving doors, I am prepared to encounter inefficiency, eccentric lack of standardization, occasional misrepresentation, and, above all, a thoughtless disregard for my time and energy.

Eddie is an ideal shopper, simple, direct and successful. No qualms, no hesitations. He loves shopping—once in six months.

He saw a sale of furniture advertised by Altman's and in twenty minutes bought a couch and five chairs. "The salesman thought I was crazy buying so much so quickly. He said most people take weeks to buy that." Eddie has the right idea.

Saleswomen will always desert any female customer when a man jingles the cash in his pocket. The assumption is that men are professionals in making money, therefore, by a jump in logic, they are businesslike in buying. Certainly their time has a money value that is absent in a housewife's budget.

I wish that men would take over the job of purchasing for the home. As official wage earners of the family they ought to have the privilege of picking the fruits of their labor. If they were to forage for children's underwear and unidentifiable yard goods, they would raise general hell. The entire retail system would be revolutionized.

I can imagine, as I sit peaceably in my backyard, what would happen if men were the Great Consumers. They would force stores to keep abreast of the times instead of jog-trotting in a jet-speed age because ladylike customers have been unexacting.

Because I am a public relations counsel as well as a consumer, I never go into a department store without wanting to change it, to make it comfortable and pleasant from the purchaser's point of view.

No one ought to criticize, as I have done, without making a few constructive suggestions. I have therefore designed a late twentieth century store in which it would be pleasant and easy to squander money. My store, drawing on all physical and social sciences, and perhaps touching on science fiction, would make use of every technological skill in the files of modern industry. Selling would be as smooth as a Ford assembly line. Buying would be as entertaining as a good movie.

The general layout of the store would be changed in concept. Instead of being designed from the decorator's point of view, as a vice-president described her store, it would be rearranged from the customer's point of view. Objects would be grouped according to purchaser logic.

I should marry technology and psychology to display objects effectively. Display rooms, equipped with television, motion pictures, slides, robot mannequins and miniature models of ships or furniture, would be the basic sales machinery. Instead of being sent to walk around the fifth floor and the basement, the customer would be directed to Display Room 1-H where, seated on foam rubber, he would see cutlery, pots, dishwashers and towels shown to him in an electronic 3D parade.

Electronic running inventories would tell you whether it was worthwhile going further into the matter. Recorded voice descriptions would give you necessary facts.

Sample rooms, also with running inventory as to sizes, colors and materials available, would show you actual goods for closer inspection. These rooms would be clustered together in areas of function.

There would be test or trial rooms where you could actually touch things, finger a curtain, try on a dress.

A constant stream of essential information would be available throughout. Good store maps would show you clearly where to go. Timetables would tell you when showings take place. Besides running inventories that would tell you if the shoe you like is available in the color and size you want, informed men and women would know if fibre-glass curtains fade. Manufacturers would cooperate to give standard information as to size, content and quality of material. ("If you are bewildered about all these new synthetic products, we retailers are twice as muddled," the head of a chain operation told me.) Descriptive terminology would be standardized and clarified by Rudolf Flesch of Columbia and S. T. Hayakawa of The University of Chicago. I can poke melons to see if they are right, but I cannot push the gleaming wall of a diswasher to make sure that it is ripe, mechanically speaking. Everything would be stated accurately and politely, because cybernetics would probably oversee management. All these things you might call the machinery of selling.

The sales force, which today puzzles management and frustrates customers, would be broken down into diversified functions. At the top of the scale would be advisers and information experts to tell you what sort of merchandise would best fit your purposes. To take over the duties that now divide the clerk's time, energy and attention, there would be experts in special areas to advise on quality, style, durability, color; there would be order takers, sales clinchers, who would dictate your order to typists; there would be expediters, telephonists, stenographers, electronic teletypists, robot errand girls, collectors of garments from try-on booths. The system would do the selling, checking and recording. There would be no salesclerk in the present sense of the word.

Fortifying the sales effort would be special services to shoppers: checking coats and packages, comfortable chairs everywhere, polite handling, no waiting because science and technology would remove distances and systematize complexities.

No customer would get up from her comfortable chair, collect her coat at a checking booth and leave the store in a tantrum or a doldrum. Even if she had bought nothing, which is unlikely, she would have had an enjoyable afternoon attending a combination World's Fair and fashion show without walking more than she cared to.

I think many women, like me, would like to have present-day shopping difficulties mitigated. But I do not dislike shopping *per se*. I have no aversion to looking at the material splendors gathered from all over the world and spread out for my visual pleasure. Never has it been possible to see so many beautiful objects displayed for one's delight and stimulation, and I might add, in so many shops. Glistening scarves from India. Enamelware, sweetly utilitarian, from Scandinavia. Silver from Mexico. Silk from Italy. Hand-woven wool from North Carolina. Ceramics from Picasso, as if he were a place instead of a phenomenon.

I should love to shop if I had unlimited time and energy, if taste and desire were the criteria of choice. All these ifs. If department stores were adjusted to my human needs, I think shopping would be fun; stores would sell more and I would buy more.

CHAPTER SEVEN

To Market

Three women and a goose make a market.
Italian Proverb

"The grocer is on fire," one of the kids yelled, so we all ran to the corner to watch the ugly store burn up. We did not for a minute think it was Mike himself, just the store. My cousin Denise and I shoved into the crowd at the corner of Third Avenue and 48th Street and saw a small smoky blaze in a striped awning over the fruits and vegetables.

"It was a stick. It flew from the Windsor Hotel fire into the awning," yelled a boy running down the street. "All the way from Fifth Avenue and 50th Street."

We went back to our homes sorry that so little had happened to the grocery.

I didn't like grocery or meat markets in 1899. I felt that marketing was embarrassing. Why did Moth have to say to the butcher, "Don't you want to cut off that end before you weigh it?" Why did anyone need to ask the grocer to tip the box of strawberries to see if the bottom berries were good and to make sure that there was no false bottom in the basket? I thought too that it was a silly way of acquiring food. I had the feeling that the grocer knew without squeezing which cucumber was good.

I knew I could never be the clever, careful and charming purchaser that I remember Moth to have been when, disconsolate and bored, I watched her bend over the vegetable stall, one hand poking a cabbage, the other hand holding up her long skirt. The grocer beamed at her as she caressed and then nibbled a plum and asked, "Three cents apiece? That's two for five, isn't it?" This pleasant practice confused me. Had the butcher asked too much or had she offered too little? Did other ladies with less charm or wisdom pay six cents for two? I knew that I would grow up to be one of the other ladies. Perhaps that is why I have not enjoyed marketing, but there are a few other reasons.

It is difficult to know what quantity will make the correct dish to set before the family.

At luncheon one day I asked an experienced housekeeper, "Do you have a system to help you calculate how much food to order?"

"Yes," she answered, as she selected shrimp from an hors d'oeuvres tray at Voisin. "It is very easy. I always order too much or I order squabs. You order one for each and one extra."

Another woman added, "When I order for guests I figure one for each, a squab or half a broiler or one filet of beef. When we haven't company and I order roast beef for the family, it is quite simple. Two ribs are plenty for three meals. Hot, cold sliced and hash."

Mary, who was making three leaves of lettuce last through the meal, said, "I never know how much food to order for guests. I can't ever predict how hungry they will be. Left-over food plagues me for a week after a party."

Fanny was coy. "In my boarding house they eat what I give them and I figure that out to the slice. I know who is going to ask for seconds."

Jane Grant said, "I have never bought the food. My goodness, if a cook can cook he can market, too. I can't be bothered."

My cook knows even less about quantity than I do, but I am willing to work on hunch. "Let's see, fifty people. Suppose we have two ducks, three tongues, two turkeys, chicken salad, green salad . . ." At any rate, my family ate leftovers for a week.

After three decades of marketing I have not learned enough to know how many portions a three-rib roast will yield.

"That's easy," my mother used to say. "You should figure a pound to a person." I have a feeling that pounds were much larger in her day than they are now. Higher mathematics today throws doubt on the inevitability of two plus two equals four. I have learned, too, that a pound of meat is relative.

Eddie, who is skeptical about kitchen scales, looked at a roasting chicken. "When you weigh this, how do you figure how much waste you should be charged for? If you don't know that, what's the use of your scales?"

It was staggering, but true. How much waste do you expect on any cut of meat? How much of bone at 98¢ a pound do I get with my 98¢ a pound of beef? Certainly I have never been told how much a three-pound chicken should weigh net.

"Madam," says my cook, "the slip says eleven and one-half pounds, but I weighed it and it's only nine pounds." We then have a fruitless discussion about the weight of waste, and I promise to remember to ask the butcher to send along what he cuts off.

"Do most of your customers know much about food waste?" I asked the butcher one day.

He smiled. "Not really. That leaves it up to me and I do the right thing for them. That's the way I like it. When they say they want a roast for six people, I know how much they should have. When they tell me they want two or three ribs I know they are usually wrong."

This is the waste chart he made out for me. I cannot vouch for its accuracy nor do I bother to consult it, but here it is, for its literary value.

Animal, Cut	*Weight—Lbs.*	*Waste—Lbs.*
chicken	5	1½
turkey	20–22	4–4½
turkey	20–28	5
turkey	12–15	3
turkey	15–20	3½–4
roast beef, 1st—2 ribs	7–8	1½
roast beef, 2nd—2 ribs	8–11	2½
roast beef, 1st—3 ribs	10–12	2–2¼
roast beef, 2nd—3 ribs	13–15	3–3½
brisket of beef, 1st cut (leanest)	5	3¾ or 30%
leg of lamb	7	1½
lamb chops, rib (frenched)		50%
lamb chops, loin	3	2

He looked at me dubiously and said, "I don't think ten per cent of my customers have scales anyway."

As an experiment in waste, I bought three lamb chops at 75¢ a pound at a cash-and-carry store and three chops at 95¢ a pound at a luxury market. The economy meat at 75¢ a pound cost more because it had more fat, and, furthermore, it was tough. It would simplify marketing if the percentage of waste were stipulated on a fair-trade basis. I should like to buy all meat in a net-weight package.

I find myself running out of tact in calling attention to errors on sales slips. "Would you mind putting the weight and cost per pound on the slip?"

"Gee, I'll try to remember, but it's so many years since somebody asked us to do that. I'll try, though."

I have never found out how to handle situations like this. "Coffee is 97¢ a pound today," says the clerk.

"I would like two pounds, please." "That will be $2.08," answers the clerk. I try to multiply ninety-seven by two until I hear him snicker, "I know it should be $1.94, but we have no pound cans. We have only half-pounds and they are 52¢, so that will be $2.08."

Markets do as much as they possibly can to keep me from knowing what I am buying. They becloud quantity, quality and pricing. Scarcity of clerks makes it necessary for customers to wait in line and, when finally waited on, to be hurried through the transaction so that they cannot attend properly to the business at hand of examining the purchase and checking on quantity and price.

On my side of the counter and at home, I feel that my personality is somewhat eroded by the thought that I ought to, but don't, watch all purchases to see if unfair trade practices are part of each bundle.

There is little doubt that many men who run markets despise the housewife as a purchaser. They show their contempt by overcharging, by short-weighting, by selling fat and bone at meat prices, by slipping decayed fruit and vegetables into the paper bag. By these and a nagging continuum of indecent practices, they keep me constantly on the defensive. They believe I have no kitchen scales, that I cannot carry out a simple multiplication problem, that I know little or nothing about food values. They conclude that I am a sitting duck and they are right.

It is not altogether because of ignorance or telephone marketing that there is so often an overpriced bag of wooden nutmegs on my kitchen table. The system of caveat-emptoring is unbeatable by any normally careful watchfulness.

One woman told me that she felt as if she had delusions of persecution and progressive paranoia whenever she came from market. I promised to find out if her suspicions were warranted and invited a well-known retail food merchant to have lunch with me at the Harmonie Club.

"Do they deliberately cheat us?" I asked, hoping that he would say no. But he said, "Emphatically, yes."

My luncheon conversation with the retail food merchant

revealed to me that there is no foolproof method by which a housewife can win the battle for fair dealing. He told me sadly that many markets specialize in tricks.

"You get gypped in so many ways I don't know where to start," he said. "There's the false bag trick. They add up your items on a paper bag so you can see it, but they put what you buy in another bag so when you get home you can't check up. When you deal at a supermarket sometimes they add in somebody else's items. You should always look for a little thingumajig that tells where your listing should start."

"Are there any more tricks?" I asked, feeling somewhat ill.

"Plenty. You see a notice in a window, loin of pork, it says, at a very low figure. But when you get it home you find you have mostly bone."

"What about canned goods?"

"Cans. That's something. Take tomatoes. Cans are rated A, B and C. A is solid pack, no extra water. B has a little water. C is all sauce. You usually get charged the same for all grades. Women don't seem to know they should specify 'A.' Everybody gets gypped on tomatoes." I am quite sure that his cynicism was unjustified. Supermarkets, for instance, are scrupulous about this.

"What else?" I asked morbidly.

"Take smoked tongues. They pump them full of brine. They shrink to about one-third of their size after cooking. Ten per cent pumping is allowed by law, but somehow they get away with it.

"Also, don't get taken in by sales. Something else is raised to make up for it. Maybe they short-weigh you on string beans, so you are paying full price anyway."

As a layman I questioned other people from time to time. The advertising manager of a large establishment scowled. "What do you expect? All down the line merchandising is like horse swapping. A horse trader isn't going to tell you all the faults in his horse."

For a moment I was delighted that I don't buy horses, but my pleasure vanished at the obvious, that I am a constant purchaser of other animals.

A woman who was graduated from a school of domestic economy, as they used to call them, told me, "I have always been thoroughly fleeced in meat transactions and in other things too. I have kept house for forty years and in all that time have found only one honest market."

I discussed the problem with my mother, who, from her experience, advised, "You should do your own marketing. You have to see the quality and watch the scales."

Mrs. Catherine Carlson, a wise and frugal housewife, was less hopeful than my mother. "You get cheated just as much when you go yourself," she said. "Yesterday on my way home, I bought half a pound of liverwurst. I watched him put it on the scale, but when I got home I found three awful old gray slices instead. It's terrible."

Marketing is the opposite of soldiering. The soldier must hurry up and wait; the housewife must wait and hurry up. This may be an unconscious device to discourage the housewife from checking up on her purchases.

Can I ask the butcher not to whisk the leg of lamb off the scale before I can look at my side of the instrument, which shows the weight, and quickly multiply pounds and ounces by price per pound? I must believe what he reads as the total from his side of the scales. Would an abacus help? How can I look at the supermarket salescheck and check it against each item when I am conscious of the line of time-driven women behind me? I think it is wiser to use markets that charge food. This gives one time, if one has the time, to check each item carefully at home with the somewhat erratic help of kitchen scales.

My cook complained about a new market. "They certainly gyp you," she said excitedly. "Look at the extra fat they've stuck on your meat, that big lump they just tooth-picked in."

Nothing confirmed the pessimism of my friends about the ethical values of our markets more poignantly than the elaborate and helpful effort made by Chicago's Department of Weights and Measures to protect the housewife. Mr. Irvine Levy, the City Sealer, sent me, in answer to my request, a large batch of material with a letter that said, "True protection cannot be had unless the housewife knows how to get her full weights and measures or exactly the amount for which she pays. It was for this reason that we embarked on a campaign to tell the housewife how to buy and assure herself of full weights and measures."

Chicago's pamphlets warned the housewife:

The merchant's scale may not be in balance.

Signs and displays may hide the scales. Get the clerk to remove obstacles.

Heavy wrapping paper and cardboard containers add weight. Pay for "net weight of the food alone."

Don't let the fish man weigh the ice with your fish. Cheap ice may cost you a lot.

Look for net weight of packaged goods.

Sales tax may be added twice.

Count your packages. You may be paying for another customer's purchases.

Look for an emblem at the top of your list on the adding-machine tape so that you are not charged for the purchases of the last customer.

My friend, the merchant, confirmed Chicago's warnings to the housewife and entertained me further.

"Do you know butchers put cooks on jobs so that they can overcharge better? That's where cooks or butlers do the marketing. The higher the bill, the higher the commission." He called these "burglar stores."

There may be an Addams-like perversity on the part of dealers, but I believe that most of the confusion on the quantity-quality-price correlation is due to the fact that scientific accounting has not yet entered this field. No one has determined standard quantity and size for a bunch of carrots. Eggs, whether they are breakfast, pullet or large, are sold by the dozen and it is hard to know whether your growing son's omelet should have one or two to make a fair bite.

"It isn't true," I protested, "that dealers throw pepper in the customer's eyes to keep them from seeing what goes on."

"How is that?" he said, evidently shocked at my optimism.

"Part of the fault is ours," I insisted. "We simply don't know what we are trying to buy when we order."

I want to believe in people's honesty. If I cannot trust my good friend, Joe, to omit a few rotten apples, how can I believe in the good faith of delegates to the United Nations? When I find that the cashier has added two dollars to my slip three days in a row, how can I reassure myself that governments are honest?

Ethics begin in the home, I realize. However, in one important facet of my life I have adjusted myself to a standard that I disapprove of but condone as inevitable. I try to dodge being fooled as if it were a game that had no relationship to morals or principles. Each mistake, I can assure myself, is an accident and exception. There is nothing I can do about it except be sworn in as an honorary member of some mayor's temporary clean-up committee.

Marketing, nevertheless, starts my day most pleasantly with a phone call. The grocer discusses classical music with me and the manager tells me about his farm and general market trends before we get down to business. "Walter, I don't mean to sound sexy, but I need an old hen with large breasts." Walter, in turn, calls me "dear" several times. I do not say, as I might have if I were forty years younger, "Oh, you say that to all the girls."

As we talk I jot down prices and quantities in my menu book and compare slips from the market with yesterday's listing. I can read my own writing, but I cannot make out the faded blue carbon marks of the clerk, usually written in an original and mystic shorthand, that reads two "Csp" and "Whrcs."

I had to ask the baker why he charged me for twelve chocolate eclairs.

"I am very sorry," he apologized sincerely. "We forgot who bought them so we thought we would try you." This was very embarrassing to me, but fortunately not to him.

I have had little success over the years in saving time and effort. I have tried to buy staples in quantity, but cans have bulged, burst and leaked. The president of a packing company gave me this advice: "Never buy fruit with a large pit in it. The sterilizing process cannot penetrate." "There is a date line on each can," he said in answer to my question, "but it is in code not meant for the public." Eddie, I am sure, would start a movement among consumers that might result in a law requiring an expiration date line on each can.

I have also tried ordering food once a month, then once a week, then twice a week, on a basis of menus made up in advance. But that, too, was costly because there were too many leftovers.

"Women can't be that systematic about the kitchen," said a friend. "My husband does all the marketing," she explained. "He loves it and he does it infinitely better than I could." I looked at Eddie thoughtfully and wondered if there was any way to induce him to take over the job which I do so inefficiently.

Clearly the job of marketing is not right for me. The value of my alleged feminine intuition is neutralized by my alleged female sensitivity. As a woman I am, by definition, too gentle to engage in a daily fencing bout with occasionally thoughtless, but usually gallant, purveyors.

Men are, by birth, by myth or by training, tough. They have been responsible for business ethics and would therefore be able to raise the level of market ethics, if they saw the need for it, through intimate daily contact with the family market basket.

Eddie only buys for fun. He likes oddities in large quantities, such as two dozen bottles of pickled onions. He sent Dorie and Annie three dozen cans of anchovies at college. Despairing calls came in collect from Wellesley and Radcliffe, "Mommy, what shall I do with them? Can I send them back?"

He believes that it is foolish and extravagant to market for bargains. "How can you spend an hour to save ten cents on a roast beef? Your time is too valuable." I can never decide whether this is good for my morale or bad for my morals.

If Eddie and other men were to take over the job of kitchen purchasing agent, they would, I hope, go about it in a professional way. They would have all items charted, standardized, categorized, sized and graded. Purchasing would be done on a competitive bidding basis.

Shopping news would be sold in weekly tip sheets, something like Kiplinger's or Corbalay's. These would cover the general food situation for immediate and future buying guidance, so that one could know whether to wait for a large pig crop or ignore grapes because they have been too heavily sprayed.

All these and many other improvements would come from masculine organizing know-how. Certainly Eddie, after fighting existing market conditions as an individual for a few days, would organize a committee of outstanding consumers, economists, bankers, educators and publicists to throw light on practices not in the public interest, with the purpose of bettering them.

As I discussed these possibilities with Eddie, who stood looking out of the window, he interrupted me, "Quick, Dorie, look. There she is again."

It was indeed the handsome, tall, stately young woman whom we have watched daily for years, carrying heavy bags of food, carrying them as if she were an Arab with a jug of wine on her shoulders, or a Powers model with a book on her head.

"Who eats all that food she carries all day long?" Eddie wondered, and so did I.

I was amazed at her endurance. How can she carry bundles weighing at least thirty pounds?

It would seem to me that the physical labor of marketing is unsuited to the frail sex. I know that all over the world women consider shopping difficult and tiring. It would be logical, on the basis of physical, emotional, psychological and economic grounds, to turn this job over to men since it calls for superior strength and endurance. In earliest times a man was the provider. He staggered home with the food on his back. Today men provide only the symbol of provisions—their earnings.

Can we hope that men will resume their ancient burden? Perhaps not. In view of men's genius for direct action, I am afraid that we should hear from time to time of a masculine marketer leaving his office, his operating theatre, or his lathe early in the afternoon and going home to change into his hunting skins. He would arm himself with bow and arrow, go around the corner and shoot a butcher for dinner.

CHAPTER EIGHT

Knife and Fork Judgments

A Goos in Hogepotte

Take a goos, & make hure clene, & hacke hyre to gobettys and put yu a potte & Water to, & Seethe togederys; than take Pepir & Burnt brede, or Blode & boylyd, & grynd to-gederys Gyngire & Galyngale, & temper uppe with Ale, & putte it ther-to; & mynce Onyonys, & freye hem in freyshe grece, & do ther-to a porcyn of Wyne.

Early English Recipes, M. Webb. Selected from the Harleian Ms. 279, about 1430 A.D.

Most girls today start along the road to a man's heart waving a cookbook whose recipe begins, "Take one meat pie from your freezer." Different from Grandma's cookbook which advised, "Take twenty-eight eggs."

Grandma was a fine cook, my mother said. I can remember only her French crullers, soft, crumbly, with powdered sugar that whitened my blue serge middy blouse; her substantial German coffee cake, a little buttery for my taste; and her bread, lumpier, I thought secretly, than the loaf delivered warm and fresh by the baker on Second Avenue. My grandmother obviously had learned nothing from her mother; and her great-great-grandchildren, who are my children, learned nothing from me.

I saw Moth cook only once. It was on an August day in the late nineties and the wonderful smell of two fresh-baked huckleberry pies filled the hot kitchen of our cottage on Staten Island. I yearned over the thick bed of glistening purple berries. Moth came to look, too.

"I can't understand it," she said. "I can't make it out."

"What?" I wanted to know, brushing flies from my hand.

"There are no flies on those pies." We studied this strange phenomenon. Moth scooped up a few berries, tasted daintily and made a face.

"Oh, goodness, I put in salt instead of sugar!"

Because desserts were indispensable, Moth served the pies and waited for the polite laughter of our guests. I had learned two invaluable lessons. Don't use salt instead of sugar. And if you have made a mistake, don't be embarrassed.

I learned nothing, almost nothing about food from my mother, because she, it seems, thought that my tennis, basketball and music were far more important than the arts of housewifery. I believe she had learned nothing from her mother.

What I learned from Moths' cook was not too constructive: how to roll pie dough, how to lick cake batter from a stirring spoon, how to turn the ice-cream freezer on a Sunday morning until the peach chunks were too cold and hard to eat.

I knew more about food than most of my friends because I had edited cooking recipes as assistant Woman's Page editor of the New York *Tribune*. But this brief literary acquaintance with the skillet was too remote from the realities of the kitchen to be of any importance or value.

If a Martian Clementine Paddleford, bored with an exclusive diet of Canal herbs, were to hop to our earth for a few ideas, she would know more about terrestrial food in a week than I have learned in half a lifetime of eating, watching, bossing and bluffing. I started as a housekeeping illiterate, and today I am less wise in the ways of pot and palate than my grandmother a century ago, possibly because my parents really didn't care much about food, especially my father, who was an almost disembodied idealist. Food was materialistic and didn't matter. I think he never knew what he was eating except for spinach and rhubarb, which had a moral connotation. He insisted that spinach should be natural, long, slimy and bitter. Rhubarb should be unsweetened, but Mother cheated. I knew nothing about psychology then, but I wonder, when he ate these hair-shirts, whether he was suffering from what now might be described as masochism and puritanism.

It seems to me in retrospect that as family caterer I have been concerned not with a cut of meat in the pot and a dollop of vegetable in a pan. I have concentrated in a scattered way, on who likes what, on who has been trained or conditioned to eat what, on who is allergic to what, for what physical or psychic reasons, on who is a whimsical child or unreasonable adult about what food. Anything can go into a cooking utensil from crab to oxtails. But what should be served for the vestibule of whose psyche? These have been the engrossing questions.

I should have known how the dining table is influenced by economics, politics, distribution, labor relations and agronomy. I know as little about why people eat what they do as I know about food itself and its preparation, as little as I know today about how food finds its way into the attributes of the body.

I have heard scientists discuss the societal aspects of eating—culture patterns, biology and geographical habits, taboos, compulsions, rituals, religious, political and social institutions, interpersonal relations, individual frustrations, aspirations, tensions and desires. All these considerations, they say, dictate what type of food any individual will eat at what time of day or year.

Modern technology has made possible a selection of food that would have challenged the imagination of H. G. Wells. Refrigeration and rapid transportation have almost wiped away limitations of season and geography. I am a magician who can produce almost anything to eat, at almost any time. But I don't. Like most of my friends, I rest comfortably on the bosom of tradition, because it is easier, and I don't know enough to pioneer.

And like most of the women I know, whether they themselves cook or merely plan meals, I find myself leaning my forehead against my fist, looking into space and saying, "What will I give them for dinner tonight?" By some psychological progression thinking up menus becomes increasingly difficult and boring with practice.

Nestling in my purse, when Eddie and I stepped into our first home, were an imaginary license in cookery and a diploma in catering.

To celebrate our first Thanksgiving, I invited Eddie's father for dinner, promising to cook for him myself. That warmed his sentimental sense of decorum. When he arrived promptly at one o'clock, I was looking in complete bewilderment at a large pallid duck. I called Eddie.

"Look," I said. "The cookbook said twenty minutes to a pound. It weighs seven pounds and it's been in the oven two hours."

Eddie stabbed at the joint and we laughed in embarrassment as blood spurted out. Eddie's father came to the tiny kitchen to help.

"What did you stuff it with?" he asked. I told him: two whole apples. But the apples and duck had been icebox cold and I had never heard of a preheated oven. None of us knew any better.

At four o'clock we were still blood-letting the duck. Eddie's father grew happier and happier, because the bride was behaving as a new bride should. I hadn't enough sense to realize that his pleasure at my ignorance was an indictment of women.

"Eddie," I asked, "are you sorry I don't know how to cook?"

Eddie scowled. "If I had wanted to marry a cook I would have."

After a few years it seemed logical to me that I ought to learn how to cook, if I was to tell any cook what to cook. Kate Rheinstein, a writer, commander of a house and mother of three children, enrolled with me in Mrs. Lempke's cooking school. Lesson five was devoted to the long hard labor of making soup. We strained, tied greens in bags, boiled, simmered, strained again and destroyed five pounds of beef. This taught me never to ask a cook to make soup. Because we felt no soup justified all this effort, we decided that further lessons were unnecessary.

My daughters knew when they set up housekeeping with their tolerant husbands that they were going to be their own cooks. Dorie and Dick live co-operate with six friends in their Cambridge home. Each person takes the job he likes best. Dick is wonderful at fried eggs and bacon for breakfast. Dorie sits by the toaster. Jack, an architect, builds good strong coffee. Mary, a psychologist, is a vegetable specialist. Dorie has stuck to her wonderful herb-flavored stew. They take turns in marketing, picking up bundles, stowing them on shelves, in the deep-freeze, penultimately in ovens and finally in the material body, which must at last be served.

A quarter of a century ago Jane Grant, her husband Harold Ross, R. Hawley Truax and Alexander Woollcott had a similar co-operative home at 412 West 47th Street. They had individual apartments, but shared kitchen, dining room and the services of a couple.

Jane was in charge of housekeeping, and she told me her most difficult job was trying to cope with Woollcott's temperament. "It drives you crazy trying to please temperamental people with different tastes," she told me. "Ross had ulcers and I had to give him bland food. But Alec wanted heavy, rich food. Fried things. Creamy desserts. Rice pudding he liked best. My goodness, puddings. All kinds of puddings. He was terrible. Ross and Hawley like clear broth. Alec wouldn't sit down to table until the soup course was finished, because he hated soup."

Annie and Justin started their marriage by deciding to live spiritually on a lettuce leaf and a cold egg. However, demands of the body will conquer them, too, I believe, because a letter from Anne in Rome (honeymoon Rome) informed us that "Joe is very cute and is developing a tremendous appetite."

When she came back she decided to take cooking lessons.

"Whatsa matter, can't you read?" asked her friend Billie.

That settled it. Anne kept her editorial job and opened her cookbooks. I suspect that, at first, everything was cooked in wine.

Grandma's good cook produced traditional meals of soup, vegetables, potatoes, salad, dessert, much like the average household or *table d'hote* menu today. My parents' meals followed a weekly routine. On Sunday, roast beef or roast chicken. Tuesday, pot roast, a dish we all disliked but about which only my brother Leon dared complain. Wednesday was steak night. Pop got the tenderloin, of course. I hid tough balls of half-chewed meat and learned permanently to distrust tender beef. Friday's fish was bony, but inevitable.

The astonishing thing about food is its cultural tenacity. And the astonishing thing about me is that I connive at being a link in the chain of tradition. I am horrified at the knowledge that my great-great-grandchildren may some day be eating replicas of meals my great-grandmother had copied from her mother.

I have seen food customs change as if they were fashions in clothes. But as in clothing, the basic facts remain. Sometimes waistcoats are fancy, sometimes waistlines are up and sometimes skirts are long. Sometimes feminine modesty is high on the chest and sometimes high on the legs. Food may be high in proteins, high in eye appeal, low in quantity, low in satisfaction. Change is superficial and usually temporary.

I have no doubt that there is some positive correlation between the two fashions. Some day someone will work it out and we shall have a new vocabulary, a new categorization and a new sub-social science.

We are anthropological slaves, and cannot deviate much from the social pattern. After the first World War, it was bathtub gin. After the Korean conflict it was gin and tonic. One day I coaxed a cook to make green-pea ice cream and use a standard recipe, but she added pistachio flavoring and sugar. The result was unspeakable. I still think that a properly made vegetable ice cream is a beautiful idea for a hot summer night. I wish some competent woman would try it.

I saw the same inflexibility in Vienna in 1923, at the Cobenzl, an old castle of Moorish-Gothic rococo design, high on a hill looking down on Vienna. I ordered wiener schnitzel and string beans. The waiter said angrily, *"Das geht nicht."* I asked why it didn't go. He answered in German, "With veal cutlets go noodles." I fought with him for an hour and accepted the noodles.

At a dinner one night a woman pushed away a plate of beets and said rudely, I thought, "Beets are for cattle." We cling to customs that dictate whether or not we shall like or abhor grasshoppers, beetles, rattlesnake meat, raw fish, raw oysters, viscera, milk or other interculturally moot foods. You can change eating habits of individuals only with a good deal of public education. Each group thinks its own foods and eating habits are right, and others' are strange, unwholesome, degenerate, anti-social or evil.

The young son of a neighboring farmer near Litchfield, Connecticut, looked at the salad and string beans we gave him for lunch, and asked suspiciously, "What's those?"

"Don't you ever eat vegetables?" my children wanted to know.

"Uh-uh," he replied. "We only eat potatoes and mush."

To introduce Dorie and Annie to alien foods, I took them

and their friends to a foreign restaurant each Saturday. They were enchanted by stuffed grape leaves in a Greek restaurant, by sukiyaki in a Japanese, soup in melon in a Chinese, zucchini in an Italian. I believe they were prepared to examine other alien ideas and accept them if they were good. If the way to a man's heart is through his stomach, an easy step to international understanding may be through the palate.

It wasn't until life grew unsettled in the twenties that I became aware for the first time that food has broad social and economic implications. Surely these and a hundred intangibles of group and personal attitudes are the crucial ingredients of the dishes a woman serves her family. Wealth, depression, war, peace, social security—these are the real lords of the kitchen. The expanding economy of the late twenties was marked by appalling prosperity menus. The boom was celebrated in every dining room. At incredibly tedious dinner parties hosts and guests gorged, compulsively or defensively, on bas reliefs in caviar, and seven-course dinners of entrée, soup, lobster, a roast, possibly crown of lamb or that unpalatable fowl, guinea hen, five or six vegetables, salad. Homemade candy baskets filled with ice cream were followed desperately by cheese and fresh fruit. Vintage wines in proper sequence were poured reverently into crystal gardens of glasses. I shudder to think of all the banquets I designed in our home, of all the feasts I endured in other people's homes.

We filled our country house with guests on weekends. On Sunday, forty-five guests fished for pike and bass, and picnicked on hot filet of beef sandwiches, or boneless squab chickens, and pails of ice cream. In the afternoon bowls of punch filled in the two-hour feeding schedule and toward evening, hundreds of minute sandwiches with cocktails. Buffet supper at eight was a Brueghel feast. Wealthy people ate gargantuanly. They seemed to get drunk on food. Anyone who served that way today would be considered insane.

While many people during the depression stood shivering in lines leading to soup kitchens, those who survived the economic debacle seemed to think they had to prove their solvency in every possible irrational way. Even families whose budgets had shrunk to a sharp point of anxiety felt it necessary to provide guests with the luxuries that had wearied palates in the preceding decade. Suckling pigs were served in state by those about to vanish from the competitive social scene. Hostess gowns accentuated the pride of women who pretended they had not cooked crab gumbo themselves. You never knew at this period whether you were going to be fed truffles or turnips. Black tie in the invitation was no clue at all.

When war brought rationing in, my children believed it was fair and right. No one complained of food, except once when Doris and Anne had a few school friends for lunch. They looked at the meat with polite suspicion. "What is that, Mommy?" Anne asked. "Alligator tail soufflé," I assured her. The girls tasted it and looked at me reproachfully. I admitted that the butcher had had only lungs that day. The girls were squeamish.

The British set us a good example. When an Englishman had lunch with us in the winter of 1943, I asked him what food he missed most at home. "Orange juice," he answered promptly. "You know, all our oranges go to the babies." I squeezed nine oranges into a highball glass. He drank it as if it were a spiritual fact.

Rationing ended, price ceilings floated away, but the new simplicity in food and service remained. Exotic foods had vanished with household help and finger bowls. At the top of the list were goulash, *arroz con pollo* and other one-dish meals, all easy, cozy and satisfying.

When President and Mrs. Roosevelt served hot dogs to England's King George VI and Queen Elizabeth, they made a great point in favor of inner security expressed outwardly in terms of food. They had no need to impress special guests.

Cecile Sorel, flamboyant French actress, impressed people by not eating. "Always dine before a dinner party," she advised me.

"Why?" I asked, trying not to see her long fingers, crimson-lacquered to the second knuckles, her brilliant red hair or the artistically camouflaged ancient cheeks. It was difficult to find any point on her person that was not embarrassingly controversial.

"Because people are more important than food. You cannot do justice to your dinner partner if you are thinking of what you are eating."

Eating in restaurants demands peculiar conformity and special talents. In Paris long ago I watched Americans cringe before waiters when they ordered a salad or an omelet. I hate rich dishes, such as filet of sole Marguery, but I was afraid to order simple dishes until I was patriotically stirred. Lunching alone at the Divan one day, I vengefully ordered an artichoke without sauce, *fraise du bois* and a glass of beer. The waiter's eyes widened. He whispered to other waiters, who lined up to study me. The chef himself, in tall white hat, pushed through the kitchen door and bowed to me, who apparently was a gourmet, a connoisseur. I am not always so lucky in finding the exact point where reverence for tradition intersects reverence for individualism.

Most of our eating habits, whether we are Hindu, Catholic, Moslem, Italian, Hungarian, Indonesian or Mexican are set when we are children, and they are altered only with great difficulty.

My generation was ruled by myths: no milk after fruits, no water after watermelon, soft-boiled eggs were more digestible than hard-boiled, lobster and ice-cream eaten at the same meal would make you deathly sick.

I have very few childhood kitchen memories, which explains perhaps why I am fairly indifferent to what I eat or how it is cooked. My own family in a lavish era ate very little and I cannot remember anyone saying, "This is good," "This is awful." Your plateful, whatever it was, was inevitable. Obedience in eating, as in everything else, was absolute when Eddie and I were children. In Eddie's family, children who didn't eat all their food were sent from the table in disgrace.

It is instructive to watch adults who were forced to eat in childhood. Eddie, usually paternal toward women, piled food on the plate of the headmistress of a girls' school. He replenished it as fast as she finished. Finally, she begged, "Please, Eddie, don't give me any more. I was brought up to clean my plate, and I've been full for the last three helpings." I can imagine Freud and Pavlov arguing over her head. "A conditioned reflex," a gloating Pavlov would say as he wiped drops from his dog's mouth. Freud would murmur, "The repetition factor is almost inescapable."

Eddie remembers oatmeal as having had heavy cream and a big dab of butter on it. "I can remember our excitement," he recalls, "when Grape-Nuts appeared; it gave you strength in some mysterious way; and Force. Sunny Jim became part of our lives. He was the first advertising personification. Milk? I can't remember ever drinking it."

My family's breakfast was, I imagine, fairly typical for New York in the 1890's: prunes, cereal, two eggs and fresh rolls delivered early by the baker. My daughters think a good breakfast is a swig of frozen orange juice.

I envy mothers of today's babies. Demand feeding seems so much more reasonable than our cruel and arbitrary schedule of waiting until the clock said we might feed our howling baby. It must be heaven to be able, with a clear conscience, to insert a bottle in a mouth that begins to open in hunger.

Annie's trained baby nurse forced her to eat while I had a cold and lay helpless, listening to her meal-time wailing through the wall. When I was no longer contagious, I had the courage to let Annie refuse milk for nearly twenty-four hours. Since that day she has never been a feeding problem.

I made sure that Dorie's and Annie's portions weren't discouragingly large. They ate only as much as they wanted. I disliked using food as reward or punishment, although I confess that I often said, "No string beans, no pudding." But never, I think, "You've been bad, no candy." When Doris was four years old, she said firmly, "I don't like spinach." Omniscient and comforting, her pediatrician, Dr. Jerome Kohn, said, "All right, beans or peas are just as good." I withheld spinach until she said, "Mommie, they have such lovely spinach at school, why can't we ever have it?"

As they grew a little older, my children learned that food can be convivial. Birthday presents, creamed chicken, ice cream, created a lovely picture of social eating. An ascetic and Spartan woman I knew gave her child's birthday guests oatmeal and milk. I wonder if that child has grown up with anorexia or ulcers, or has become a misogynist. Probably he sits alone in a corner and gnaws bones like an animal.

Our eating is much more than a physiological and cultural process. It is the result of everything that has been done to us by our society plus everything we have made of ourselves, in addition to numerous other facts and influences. Our eating shows our adjustment or, contrariwise, our desire to disturb others or hurt ourselves. Even conflicts are sometimes highlighted in the dining room.

An artist, recently married for the third time, chewed his food as viciously as if he were eating his psychoanalyst. When he snubbed his wife brutally, her eyes filled with tears, but she picked up her fork and thrust a morsel of beef between smiling lips. The silent power of her jaws answered his attack.

How often teeth in action have revealed the emotions of polite eaters. One evening, a lawyer told us his wife had alienated their son. She laughed sweetly now and then protesting, "Now, George," and, "You all know how he exaggerates."

But we knew George was right. She worked steadily at a bowl of nuts. Crunch, crunch. She was gnawing at her own bones, her anxieties, her shames, her regrets.

No doubt psychologists will before long be able to understand people by watching and classifying methods of wielding knife and fork. I can imagine a psychiatrist setting a plate of pumpkin pie before the accused and, as he eats, deciding whether the man is lying or standing on the Fifth Amendment. A personnel manager by the same test will gauge an applicant's fitness to work as a draftsman or to command men.

I enjoy making knife-and-fork judgments about people. I watched a woman slash her steak viciously and chew it as bitterly as if it were a mouthful of frustration. She wanted more out of life than fodder. Her lethargic husband methodically sank huge forkfuls into his mouth. His food nourished him, hers made her gaunt and angry.

If I knew what combination of emotions, activity and foods could give us the kind of body that aesthetes, dressmakers and doctors admire, my life as a housekeeper would be far easier. For years I have catered to a family that wants slimming food, but wants it delicious and satisfying, especially between meals.

Food is a schizophrenic fantasy. Everybody loves it, nobody wants it. How much pleasanter were the old plump days when there was no ambivalence in appetite, when two short, round music critics could invite me to Huyler's after the opera, pull themselves up on high counter stools and happily consume double chocolate ice-cream sodas. I think they had no guilt feelings.

When America started to worry about weight, strange and irrational diets swept the country. A man on Long Island lost seventy-five pounds by living on bananas and milk and racing up and down the beach all day. A distant cousin of my mother's drank vinegar secretly, and died. One lamb chop and a slice of pineapple twice a day was another grisly diet. One read about pills for slimming, pills that contained the head of tapeworms, to be taken three times a day; pills containing massive doses of thyroid; benzedrine pills; too often defeating the cause of health.

Diet books crowd the shelves of bookstores. *Eat and Grow Thin* and other depressing titles have dominated our lives. *Harper's Bazaar* was responsible for a vast, temporary decrease in weight. Hendrik van Loon one evening said proudly, "I've lost a lot of weight." Lucille Buchanan, an editor of *Harper's Bazaar,* appraised him, "Down to a ton!"

Some diets often proved so enervating that people gave them up after a week or two to get fat again. One charming friend was like a balloon, constantly expanding and contracting. She heaved herself forward and nervously crushed her cigarette in an ash tray. "I smoke to stop eating. I eat to stop smoking. This goes on until I am now smoking and eating at the same time."

An otherwise intelligent friend of ours eats everything everybody does. He also has winter raspberries flown from the South especially to make him thin. To make sure that he eats enough thinning food, he has a box of Ry-Krisp and a bowl of applesauce at his bedside table. However, his excellent tailor manages to keep his mirrored form fairly slim.

Psychiatrists today are having great fun with overeating, applying the edge of their thin-slicing category knives to see why some people remain maliciously fat. Let me list some of the reasons for overeating mentioned by an expert: Need of affection or love. Defiance of authority. Need to hold onto everything. Feeling of carrying no weight in one's group. Lack of interest in anything, and compensatory need to fill that void. Resentment and aggression, suppressed in everything except demolishment by tooth. Desire to make up for lack of height by excess breadth. Compensation for previous privation.

My own observation shows some variants from these generalities. A sweet young friend who hoped to be an opera singer ate in desperation, the symbol of a fat prima donna firmly fixed in her mind. But her voice was not good enough. Later she gave up music, adjusted to another career and grew slim.

However, I have seen enough unreasonable overeating to prove the psychologic points made by doctors. An ulcerous architect bragged that his doctor told him he would die unless he stopped eating nearly everything. I have watched him eat vastly with sensual pleasure. He is repulsive to women and I suspect he has had to transfer his emotions to his food. Another man with a bad heart is a secret eater. "It is worse than being a solitary drinker," said his wife, shuddering.

After an oversumptuous dinner a psychologist held forth. "We all agree that eating is a substitute for love. If you are deprived of love, you go for another piece of pie. Now, the thing to do is to stop suppressing your ability to express love. Bring it out. Feed other people. You'll be surprised how much you love people you feed. Then, if you will let me round out the rondo, you will get so much satisfaction from watching people eat you won't need to eat yourself."

Some overeaters grow thin, as did a beautiful woman who ate continuously and ravenously and seduced hordes of men. The more she ate and loved, the thinner and hungrier she grew. Hate seems to make many people thin, but you can't count on it. I know some corpulent bodies who are quite virulent all the time.

Another thin and voracious eater was a wistful Austrian who had never recovered from wartime privation. He ate huge quantities of food in a useless effort to store up supplies against the next period of privation. The more he ate the thinner he got.

How does one get thin? Every doctor knows. Eat less. And attack the problem on the psychological front.

There is a growing rebellion among overweight dieters. Not yet a strike, mind you. Just a tendency to ask here and there what the relationship is between life-insurance statistics and some demonstrable and contradictory facts of life. Such as the woman who uses mayonnaise and remains thin and the lemon-dressing woman who stays fat. Is overweight a symptom or a cause? What do different bodies do with the same or different foods? Metabolism is probably not the whole answer. I suspect we are on the brink of scientific discovery.

Dieting would be very easy if one could say, "I'll never eat again as long as I live." It may be easier to be cured of alcoholism than to be cured of eating, and safer.

Catering to idiosyncrasies, whether they are neurotic, antisocial, archaic, tribal, or merely ridiculous, is fun and often is challenging. I am always surprised at the vagaries and eccentricities men, women and children can develop about food.

I dislike strawberries. When I was quite young, I spent wistful summer hours embroidering large silken strawberries, beautifully shaded from crimson to celadon, pitted with careful French knots, and surrounded by spiked emerald leaves. Today a strawberry tastes as sharp as the needle that bit my finger at every stitch.

Eddie likes any food cold from the icebox better than he likes it hot at the table, even cold mashed potatoes when he thinks his weight can afford it.

I suppose the reason why women pamper prejudices and favor real needs is because it satisfies the maternal drive.

That is why I enjoy remembering that Charles Hodges prefers brandy, Voz Lyons likes a drop of grenadine in soda, Fannie Hurst favors poached eggs and Mary Kennedy, the poet, likes tea at tea time.

Ed Whitman is so wild about hash that we roasted beef

one afternoon and ground it up, hot and fresh, for dinner. I thought it was vandalism until he said, "This is heaven." Dorie loves zucchini and alligator pears, Dick likes bitter chocolate, Annie likes marshmallows on her sweet potatoes, Marguerite Clark likes the end piece of roast beef. Pat Partridge loves boiled beef and so does Olga Knopf, the psychiatrist who drools when she talks about *Bein-Fleisch,* which I have never tasted. She was sympathetic when she heard that we had always arrived too late at her favorite restaurant in Vienna to get this mysterious shin-bone stew. "All gone," said the waiter. Mme. Pandit liked *marrons glacés* so much she took a second spoonful for her ice cream.

In the summer of 1923, Eddie asked me to bring to his Uncle Sigmund a dozen tins of G. Washington coffee and a crate of fresh grapefruit. His gratification was sobering. It seemed incredible that this great man in Vienna should lack the commonplaces of the American chain store.

Wondering what visitors from overseas will like is an exhilarating and hazardous sport. I guessed that Daisy Walwyn on a visit from Africa would like Brussels sprouts. She sighed deeply as she slowly lifted a few onto her plate. "Brussels sprouts. How nice. It does bring back memories of my childhood in England. You know we can't grow it in Africa. It's a good vegetable. It's sturdy and honest. It's just itself. It mustn't be disguised. It's a romantic vegetable." We were moved by her anthropomorphic and moral appreciation of this much maligned little cabbage. Kamakshi Sundaram, a beautiful physician from India, is a vegetarian, and we loved finding new combinations to please her and tempt her small appetite.

It is not amusing to take care of people's dislikes. People who hate foods usually hate to be tactful, like the man who said rashly just before dinner that he hated all red meat. I had to do a little back-of-the-scenes whispering, but I saw him weep into a plate of scrambled eggs as a thick steak passed him by. Eddie thinks he dislikes leg of lamb but eats it with surprised pleasure whenever it is served. Each time he thinks it is only uniquely good. I learned to test his distastes after years of believing them immutable.

Fortunately I have not had to do much about food for invalids. The whole idea of feeding people who can't or shouldn't eat irritates me a little, perhaps because Moth made me drink orange juice when I had the mumps and was too young to protest that it hurt.

I was enraged when my household tried to make me eat when I had pneumonia. I had never complained about food before, so when I started yelling, "Take that garbage away," Eddie telephoned the doctor. My sister had pneumonia soon after and was delighted when I told her how to handle people who tried to make her eat. All day long this gentle woman vetoed trays, "Take that garbage away."

Although sick-bed feeding has fortunately been rare in my life, there always seems to be one person at table who can't eat what everyone else has, and others who shouldn't eat normal food, but do. Some diabetics, for instance, require special food, while others merely want sympathy and admiration for their ailment.

Most frustrating of all are the unpredictable guests with ulcers. You offer them milk. "Thanks," they will say with a pleasant scowl, "I just drank some before I came here." You present them with puréed vegetables, as suggested by their wives that morning. "Nonsense," they will say, shoving the plate away and reaching for cucumber salad.

Allergy is the fifth dimension of hospitality. Marguerite sneezes at chrysanthemums in the center of the table. Loraine Sobel gets deathly sick if there is an onion in her food, so we edit carefully for her. Jack shudders if he so much as sees a fish. But Anne now enjoys all the foods she couldn't eat when she was a hay-feverish child.

I enjoy the vagaries of occasional guests because I like

variety in everything, but it is in the day-to-day occupation of devising menus and divining market supplies and managing kitchen and pantry personnel (sometimes hired and sometimes just myself, but all somewhat aboriginal) that I have failed to improve my mind, my skill, my knowledge or my character. I have always felt several centuries behind the needs of our current household. I cannot catch up with the antique arts of the table.

One important lesson I learned from my mother was that unexpected guests are fun and that they can be fed without excitement, fuss, or difficulty. This came to me not by precept, but by example. For instance, we knew, my brothers, my sister and I, that we could ask as many of our friends as we wanted for Sunday-night supper. We helped set the table and we went out and bought the food.

Moth said, "Here is four dollars." Usually a boy went with me to the delicatessen store around the corner from our house on 107th Street near Riverside Drive. His job was to help select and carry the banquet that one could buy for four dollars. The store was cheery, leisurely and redolent. The counter was decorated with cold cuts still fresh and warm. I wish I knew today where to get such fresh-baked, yeasty bread on a Sunday night.

My problem was going to be how to organize. I thought it was going to be only a matter of psychology, how to deal with people.

But when we moved into our big house on Washington Square from our small Washington Mews home I did not realize that I was about to become a restaurant keeper on a large scale, serving our guests the elaborate formal meals of the orgiastic twenties. I believed our new home would run itself just as easily as had our first one. All that was necessary, I felt, was to get competent servants and let them run the show.

But they all had to be fed and the food thought of by me.

No housekeeper to take this chore from me, and give me more time to help take care of our two children and work at our office. My formula was simple. I would hire a good cook and a good butler and everything would be perfectly all right. I was lucky.

Margareta was an enormous Dutch woman who had been known in Holland as a *Koch Demoisel.* She looked like Queen Wilhelmina and was proud of it. We had daily conferences at 8:30 to discuss menus and to hear the story of her life. She loved to see her large kitchen piled up with mountains of food. Her childhood must have been hard, because she hoarded bread until it grew mouldy.

Bahnesen brought great professional skill and intelligence to his career as butler; he remembered guests' names, their likes and dislikes and idiosyncrasies. He served with the flair of a Toscanini.

Twenty-two guests for dinner four times a week and twenty additional people for a hot midnight snack presented problems that I faced with closed eyes.

As I looked back on it, I wonder how I had the stamina or courage to wage my solo battle, unequipped as I was with knowledge or tools. I had no managing housekeeper. I struggled, unaided, in a welter of servants, menus, markets, bills and guests. I suppose it was the variety of jobs that kept me from breaking under the weight of my ignorance. Luckily, there was no time to brood over my incompetence for my high position of *maitre d'hotel.*

"I like to be a guest at my own dinner parties," I boasted, but it didn't work out that way. I have never been completely relaxed at a party in my own home. I have tried to ignore everything but extraordinary events, like the explosion of a set of ruby-red glass octagonal plates which Eddie had just bought. Ten guests helped themselves to ice cream and a series of sharp reports rang from end to end of the table. Every plate parted neatly down the middle, as in a nightmare. The plates had not been pre-cooled. Philippe of the Waldorf knows that trick. His ice-cream plates are ice-cold and his brandy snifters are warmed.

Fortified by almost complete ignorance of materials and methods, I divided my food problem into three categories: food for my children, food for the personnel, and food for guests. I paid no attention to the way Margareta produced Baked Alaska or candy baskets, but I did go down to the basement kitchen every day to make sure that she scraped beef properly for Doris and Anne.

Nine employees could be counted on to eat about 180 meals a week, counting days off, so it seemed a good idea to handle that problem on a mass-production basis, to save time and energy. I dictated their menus for four weeks at a time, made out a purchasing schedule for the entire period and mailed my order to Washington Market which made deliveries to us two or three times a week. Staples, such as soap, flour, sugar, were ordered in quantity and stored away. In this way I crammed all my steady customers into a morning's work once a month. These menus seem pretty strange to me today. Why, for instance, did I specify chicken à la king on Sunday, and roast beef on Monday? And I wonder what happened to leftovers.

My daughter Doris, who has now kept house for over four years, seems to have more knowledge about food and a greater affection for it than I ever had.

She said to me with great wisdom, "If you actually prepare the food yourself, clean it, scrape it, chop it, broil it, put it on plates, you have more of a feeling of *giving* than you do when you ask someone else to do these things." She was right, of course. But not for me.

When I was four years old, my mother descended to the kitchen and to her horror saw me eating a boiled egg that only I could have cooked because I was alone in the kitchen. She smoothed me over her knees and gave me the only spanking she ever administered. "You know you're not allowed to go near the stove." When she found out I had not cooked the egg, she gave me a penny to indemnify my wounded ego. To this day I still believe in justice as she dispensed it. And to tie up everything nicely, I have always been too busy to cook.

I like to believe that I love to cook, but I am much too lazy to go through the chores of washing and scraping, putting things into pots, lifting pots in and out and off and on again. And I am much too impatient to wait for things to grill and broil and brown.

We dined at the home of a true gourmet, Robert Craig, in Honolulu and watched him prepare dinner. A charming American girl of Japanese descent followed him like a golf caddy, washing each pan after he had used it.

"I wouldn't cook," he said, "if I had to wash up."

"How would you like to cook regularly?"

"Perish the thought," he said, waving a copper pot full of sauce. "I wouldn't ever do routine cooking." He added thoughtfully, "My wife does that."

Does eating together promote good family relationships? That is the theory, but I have seen many dining rooms that served as emotional wrestling arenas. Some ulcers, it would seem, come from the restive board and not from the pressure of work and worry. Perhaps the family should meet socially after eating quietly in separate nooks. And as for social dining with a large S, I can imagine nothing better designed to build up misanthropy.

As I look back on thirty-three years of sustaining, gratifying and surely overfeeding a family and countless guests, I am amazed how little I know about the essence of food, its thingness, its *ding-an-sich*. Is food a first cause? What lies back of its obvious function of adjusting chemical balance, of supplying excess energy that short-circuits into all sorts of mischief?

And I wonder at the choice of values open to any housewife. Her choice is frighteningly important to the world of eaters and producers. To the world of international politics, of finance. To the inner life of all people.

I should like to have a university research group do a scientific study of eating habits and food preparation, to examine every idea on the subject, to take nothing for granted, to test all our assumptions about eating. Are our routines, our conceptions as to basic needs really inevitable and good? Or would it be well to modify them now, or wait for the day when we shall have to, as many scientists predict?

For my part, I look forward to an evening meal of a nice conch shell full of plankton soup.

Certainly men engaged in cooking and catering professionally have nothing to add to the oldest of crafts. They prefer to carry on pretty much as their mothers did at home, with an occasional invention in sauce, just enough to let them feel creative.

I should like to be a farmer and feed pigs cloves to save cooks the bother of decorating a ham; I would feed my chickens curry and send them to my Indian friends; feed my lambs onions and garlic to be ready for stew or roast; irrigate my apple orchards with cinnamon; and, if I were at the seashore, grow clams in Boston's milk.

Human animals, like other species, spend far too much time stuffing themselves with the human equivalent of grass and worms. Wouldn't it be wonderful if we could eat noble thoughts by photosynthesis and breathe them out as good deeds and clear words?

I wonder at the temerity of writing about my concern with too much food, knowing that the major portion of the world's population is used to having far too little food. Here is the eternal conflict between natural production, human appetite and economics, whether it is in Singapore, Sicily or the Bowery.

My cousin, Edna Mann, the psychologist, made it clear to me one day. "Sometimes intelligence tests tell us more about the social pattern of the child's family than of the child's intelligence," she said. "Yesterday I showed two boys a picture of a crying child sitting at a table and a frowning woman standing beside him. Interpreting the picture, one boy said, 'He's crying because he wants more to eat, and his mother is sad because there is no more.' The other boy said, 'He's crying because he doesn't want any more and his mother is making him eat.' "

I should like to find some ultimate truth in food that explains why the lives of billions of people are used in growing, distributing, selling, buying and preparing this product. I should like to find a relationship between an underarm loaf of bread in Paris and a bowl of rice in Calcutta. Food, the tyrant of tyrants.

Five robins probed diligently at my neighbor's grass in Nantucket and a stubby rabbit nibbled and quick-pouched its cheeks, while I watched the rosy-fingered dawn between five and six o'clock. Next day a sedate family of partridges worked on this combined farm, market, kitchen, dining table as if their lives depended on it. As they did, in fact.

CHAPTER NINE

Double Your Partner

"I have taken notice, Monsieur, that people who are only in each other's company for amusement, never really like each other so well, or esteem each other so highly as those who work together, and perhaps suffer together."

Charlotte Brontë

"A woman should be good for everything at home, but abroad good for nothing."

Euripides: *Meleager,* Fragment 525

Grandma was the first career woman I knew, even though she worked only two hours a week. But there was no suggestion that this quiet, rather elegant woman, whose hair was dressed every evening by a coiffeur, had ever done a lick of useful work in her life. It was my job to console my weeping Grandpa when she died the year McKinley was assassinated.

Here we are, more than three-quarters of a century after my grandparents' world accepted their double partnership; yet many people start worrying about the future of the world when they visit my pink office a floor above Eddie's green office at 26 East 64th Street. First they worry about a threat to male supremacy, then they fret about the sanctity of the home, and then they shudder about neglected children.

I suspect that there is an underlying conviction that husbands and wives exchange sex when they work together in an office. There is usually a point at which people leer at me and seem to say, "So you wear the pants." Perhaps for this reason it is considered precarious for a businessman to permit his wife to work with him. And the danger is somehow in direct ratio to the size of the business. The wife of the cigar-stationery store husband is acceptably gracious to customers, but I imagine that stockholders would request a special meeting if the wife of the president of a billion-dollar steel corporation were made executive vice-president.

By a curious inconsistency some professions are exempt from the general rule. It has long been considered glamorous for actors, singers, writers and artists to work side by side, although I should think upsets due to temperamental clashes would be magnified here. And it is considered quite proper when sociologists like the Sheldon Gluecks of Harvard Law School combine to illuminate some of the problems of penology and juvenile lawbreaking. I have enjoyed, with no feeling of surprise, watching them supplement and dovetail each other at a conference.

The counting house, the directorate board, are the modern battlefields on which the battles of the sexes, in the Thurber sense, take place. It is on these fields that men must prove their commercio-intellectual virility. It is on these fields, where men use the hunch and women follow their intuition, that women dip their flags.

Many men, if they think at all of a female partner, do not relate her to their wife at home, their wife on a dance floor, or their wife with a bag of groceries in her arms. The woman sitting behind the executive desk down the hall is a mythical monster, a fabulous combination of steam-roller, fire engine with all sirens shrieking, a prize-fighter, a sadist, a weeper, a non-stop complainer, a sex maniac who uses all the wiles of Lilith to defeat Adam. In many a man's fancy she has the deadly poisonous charm of a snake; her eyes glitter, her mouth swings open, her tongue vibrates. Her paralyzed victim can only wait destruction.

A businessman confided to us, "I think it's great the way

you two work together," but he was really frightened at our temerity. We asked why he looked skeptical, and he answered classically, "Me? Work with my wife? I should say not; a man has to have some freedom."

Many men tend to be explosive when the discussion gets around to this subject. "Boy! She bosses me at home. That's enough for me."

"If I bawled her out, the way I can do to a man, she'd bust out crying. As it is, I can't even hiss at my secretary or she'd walk out on us."

We have strange misconceptions about women anyway, based on old myths that cling like barnacles. In spite of ourselves we half-believe them. It is hard too to brush off labels that poets, philosophers and historians have pinned on us. Judgments sometimes run in contradictory pairs. Tertullian said, "You are the gateway to the Devil"; but Tagore thought, "You are one-half woman and one-half dream." Lord Chesterfield, who felt "Women are to be talked to as below men, and above children," differed from Samuel Johnson, "Sir, nature has given woman so much power that the law cannot afford to give her more." Kipling, unusually gallant, conceded, "A woman's guess is much more accurate than a man's certainty."

In a scientific mood, Aristotle classified us in a miscellaneous file: "Woman is more compassionate than Man, more ready to weep, more jealous, more querulous, more inclined to abuse . . . an easy prey to despair and less sanguine than Man, more shameless and less jealous of honour, more untruthful, more easily disappointed, and has a longer memory . . . likewise more cautious, more timid, more difficult to urge into action, and she requires a smaller quantity of food." (*De Animalis Historia*)

He also thought that "male children are formed in the womb by the thirteenth day, females by the forty-fifth." Martin Luther's observations and conclusions were equally positive: "Men have broad and large chests, and small narrow hips, and more understanding than the women, who have but small and narrow breasts, and broad hips, to the end they should remain at home, sit still, keep house, and bear and bring up children."

Women are supposed even today to be more spiritual than men. (They have no characters at all, said Alexander Pope.) Euripides said, "Woman is woman's natural ally." But many personnel directors are sure that women hate to work for other women. "We can't have women competing for men's jobs." "Too much absenteeism." "Not steady on the job." "They get married and quit." "Too disturbing to the peace of mind of the men around them." (Can't you get somebody good-looking around here?)

Aristotle called woman an inferior man, and employment agencies thousands of years later agree with that philosopher. So do many labor unions (not officially, only practically). And so do many industrial organizations.

Myth magic works as powerfully on women as on men. For every man who says, "People would think it awful funny if my wife worked for me," there is a woman who agrees. They, too, have rationalizations as well as reasons.

People who object violently to the idea of double partnership usually believe women should stay at home anyway, where they belong (forgetting that the majority of women have to earn money outside if they and their families are to have the comforts of one square meal a day, send their children to college, and pay the doctor's bills). It is the old rivalry between the sexes that seeps into the new terrain. Jealousy. Prestige. Power. Dominance.

Eddie thinks that women are the intellectual equals of men, but emotionally he accepts the principle of male dominance. He accepts a woman's ideas as willingly as if they were masculine. "Whit, just listen to Dorie's idea." He is not afraid of losing face by having his wife share his professional life. "Have you met my partner, Miss Fleischman?"

I, too, am tradition-oriented. I disapprove strongly of my profound feelings that men should rule. My father and brother, whom I obeyed instantly, set the pattern of my attitude toward men, an attitude slightly tinged with awe. I accept suggestions more readily from men than from women because some man has always bossed me. Men, of course, have nothing to fear but their terror of feminine rivalry, and women have nothing to fear but men's fear.

Successful double partnership depends on one's attitude toward male dominance. Whatever the differences between the sexes, there is real power in the world-wide belief that men ought to boss women where they live and where they work.

Eddie's word is final and he casts the deciding vote in our partnership. I have elected him Chairman of the Board and Executive President in our personal life, where he decides where we shall live and when we shall diet, and in our public relations office where he was boss even before we were married.

Eddie was responsible for my working life long before I joined his staff in 1919. As the only reader of my high-school and college fiction, he encouraged me to want a job.

Fortunately, my father too thought that female idleness was quite unhealthy in a period when spinsters were expected to be dependent on their families. The entire tradition of his decorous Albany background was to provide protection and comfort for all women of the family. He was completely conservative in everything but his attitude toward women working. Only in this was he ahead of his time.

I was somewhat hazily sure that housewifery was not going to be my main occupation. This seemed to have been implicit all through my education. I was going to "do something" after college. Toward the end of my senior year at Barnard Pop had a talk with me. "What will you do after graduation?" He waited, and because I was too bewildered to answer he said, "I should like you to do social welfare work of some kind." I shuddered, picturing myself a Lady Bountiful carrying Thanksgiving baskets to the Dickensian poor of New York, but I answered politely, "I don't think I would be able to do that very well." (Nevertheless like most American citizens I have done volunteer work of various kinds all my life.)

"What would you like to do?"

"I would like to be a psychiatrist." I had majored in English and philosophy and also in psychology, no doubt inspired by Eddie's Freudian conversation, and by many of my friends, young doctors like Reuben Ottenberg and psychiatrists, especially Clarence Oberndorf, who told me something of what this new science was trying to do. Psychology at Barnard, unfortunately, had nothing to do with emotions or neuroses. It was physical and experimental psychology. Under Dr. Harry Hollingworth we timed reactions to pictures in advertisements, and cut up sheep eyes to examine the organ of vision. We stood in dark closets to watch complementary colors alternate.

Pop frowned at the thought of psychiatry. "That's no career for a woman. Didn't Dr. Oberndorf tell you so?" I nodded. "He said you would have to interne in an insane asylum, I believe."

Pop was clearly impatient. "What do you want to do, then? Every woman should be useful."

"I would like to go into advertising." This raised a storm from Pop, who believed in modesty, and in accurate, precise and proven truth. "Do you want to be a charlatan, a mountebank?"

I wept and Pop silently withdrew.

Neither Pop nor I suggested music although I practiced piano four hours daily and sang with all doors and windows closed lest anyone hear the high reaches of my voices. William Brady, my singing teacher, encouraged me to think of opera as a career, but because I was sure that no impresario would desire me, I had already abandoned all hope of entering this field.

It was Eddie who decided after I was graduated that I must become a newspaper reporter, like my brother Leon, who worked on the New York *World*. Eddie introduced me to Yetta Geffen of the New York *Telegram*, who was charming and helpful.

"Go to see Bessie Breuer on the New York *Tribune* and suggest that you do an interview with Mrs. Gould." Mrs. Charles Judson Gould, a wealthy woman, had sponsored a labor meeting on her estate near the city.

Mrs. Breuer smiled and said, "Try it."

When she accepted the story, she asked, "Would you like a permanent job?" I was so frightened I said, "I'll have to ask my father." Pop was pleased.

For several years, as assistant editor of the woman's page and assistant Sunday editor, I wrote feature interviews with hundreds of celebrated persons. Our woman's page, under the guidance of Helen Rogers Reid, was a leading influence in the Feminist movement and in the fight for Woman's Suffrage. Mrs. O. H. P. Belmont was a fruitful source of news in her home in New York and her fabulous marble mansion in Newport. Doris Stevens was beautiful and politically wise. Mrs. Frank Vanderlip in those suffrage days developed the organizing genius which later made her so powerful and effective on behalf of the New York Infirmary. Mrs. Carrie Chapman Catt, stern and mysterious, was a difficult source of news. She secreted Rozika Schwimmer in her apartment where I found her and got some of the background of her plans. Her story was later to convulse two continents as the tale of the Ford Peace Ship.

Irene Castle was as beautiful backstage as she was behind the footlights. Pavlova, walking through rehearsal on the Metropolitan Opera House stage, seemed never to touch the floor; her personality, too, seemed half grace and half elusive wisdom.

Margaret Sanger in 1915 was already a controversial figure, an engaging and dedicated personality. Modern social welfare was in its infancy, full of goodwill and fads. Jane Adams, Mrs. James Speyer, Mary Simkhovitch were pointing out new directions. Rose O'Neill, creator of the Kewpies, shocked *Tribune* readers when she called women "child-bearing sheep." And Colonel Theodore Roosevelt told me he was not afraid of the dark.

During this period Eddie was managing Caruso, as a partner in the Metropolitan Musical Bureau, and serving as press agent for many Broadway plays and stars. He handled the Diaghileff Ballet Russe and struggled with the growing eccentricities of Nijinsky. He edited the *Medical Review of Reviews* and the *American Dietetic Gazette*. I wrote reviews and stories for him for fun.

After his work on the Creel U. S. Committee on Public Information here and in Paris, I joined his staff in 1919 to help win recognition of Lithuania's independence. I was a professional, trained as a reporter and an editor. I knew something about Eddie's novel ideas and methods. After World War I we worked for the War Department under Colonel Arthur Woods for the re-employment of ex-service men. We handled the first NAACP convention to be held below the Mason-Dixon Line in Atlanta, Georgia in 1920.

Years later Walter White asked me, "Doris, do you know you never left your hotel without a bodyguard of four men?" I didn't know it. When I had gone to Atlanta to make advance arrangements for publicity, I visited the newspapers and suggested that they treat this convention just as they customarily treated conventions. Their calm and matter-of-fact handling helped to make the community accept this invasion from the North quietly.

But Walter White asked me, "Did you know that men

standing around the hotel threw pennies at your feet?" I didn't notice the pennies, nor would I have understood the meaning of that gesture.

Slowly, in the course of my work with Eddie, I learned that men were not altogether happy about career women. In the early days of public relations I was an exception in a masculine world. Silk and luggage manufacturers, radium miners, science institutes accepted me with polite surprise.

Gradually, however, I became one of many women who seemed to be competing with men. Barriers had to be crossed. Many men resented having women tell them what to do in their business. They resented having men tell them, too, but advice from a woman was somewhat demeaning. I learned to withdraw from situations where the gender of the public relations counsel was a factor or where suggestions had to be disassociated from gender. If ideas were considered first in terms of my sex, they might never get around to being judged on their merits. Not always, of course. The general manager of a plant whose 80,000 workmen threatened to go out on strike was delighted when I suggested that the War Labor Board should be asked to solve his problem.

However, I made no attempt a few years ago to sit in on conferences with a large trucking manufacturer that was in danger of being taxed and road-licensed out of existence. The executives were large-muscled fighters. I dared not let myself imagine their reaction if I were to tell them how to handle their drivers, or how to eliminate public prejudice against trucks. Our organization, led by Eddie, devised a program for road improvement which has now become an important national issue.

Have I been a coward to withdraw from such active company? Perhaps I have. But if I were to start in as public relations woman today, I think I would have less opportunity to share the council table than when I began this work in the early twenties.

"Don't you lose your self-sufficiency by leaning on your husband, or on the men in your organization?" a literary agent asked me.

"We all need independence," said a successful merchant. "I wouldn't be nearly so independent if I were working for my husband."

The secretary of a judge said, "I wouldn't know whether I was any good or not if I worked for my husband. I've got to prove my own value by working for someone else."

She tried to explain away my doubts. "It's important to keep the respect of your husband. If I worked for him I would be his inferior."

"Don't you feel inferior to another man who is your boss? Don't you mind that?"

"Don't be silly. Of course I don't mind. Everybody is inferior to somebody."

A young copywriter was emphatic about not joining her husband's advertising agency. "He runs me as it is. Where would I be if he could boss me in business, too? I always try to do what he likes at home. I enjoy pleasing him. Sure, every woman does. But just the same, we've got to be allowed to boss our own lives somewhere, sometime along the line."

A young housewife made another point: "If I didn't agree with him, we'd have to fight. It's all right for me to give in to little things at home when I don't agree with him. But things are important in an office, aren't they? You just couldn't give in if you didn't mean it."

A nineteen-year-old girl believed love itself was at stake. "A husband and wife should never work together. It's bound to rub off the glamour. They would just become two people. There wouldn't be any love left."

"It's not good to mix love and business," said the head of a large corporation, who was noted for his habit of mixing them.

At this point Eddie grinned at me and said, "Isn't that what I always say to you?"

A young grandmother looked cynical at this point. "It's easy for you to talk. My husband paints at home. It's such a bother having him on my hands all day." She stopped short. "Oh, I'm sorry. You work in your husband's office. Don't you get bored to death—the same man all day and all night?" If her husband bored her part of the time, he obviously bored her more all of the time.

There are some disadvantages in working with your husband. Clearly, co-operation as complex as this cannot be perfectly even. It is impossible to place everything favorable on one side of a line and everything unfavorable on the other. Occasionally I wonder whether perhaps the worst features are really the best, and the good points slightly damaging. Continuous contiguity of twenty-four-hour partnership has made me depend on his presence. Being so used to someone is good. It is also crippling. If your husband despises idleness and you like vacations you feel deprived as you swim in warm waters and relax in salty breezes. The telephone becomes as important as if it were a matrimonial umbilical cord.

You admire your partner's powers of persuasion and the force of his personality. You boast that you yourself never try to persuade anyone of anything, but you are occasionally aware of the softening of your own personality and courage.

Your traits, traditionally feminine, are emphasized; your submissiveness and your willingness to like it are nurtured. Eddie has protected me from nearly all battles, and I have not had to walk the thin line between exploiting sex and being officious. You are vaguely disturbed by his Sir Walter Raleigh attitude, but there is far more to this than a cloak flung on a mud muddle. You are never allowed in the fighting zone.

Is this good, or is it bad? Your husband, after thirty-odd

years of double partnership, admits that he wanted you not to become hardened in a tough arena. I am no fighter by nature. Eddie is. Everything hangs together in a classic picture of marital cooperation.

In Washington Eddie looked at me scornfully. "What are you afraid of? Tell them they are sabotaging their own committee. There's no use in pussyfooting. You're there to give them advice."

"If I know it won't do any good, why should I fight?" Why should anyone fight, I wonder.

Eddie groaned, "That's what you always think. Why do I ever listen to you?" He grinned. "Women!"

In the course of years we have, not surprisingly, had a few clients who were too gallant to talk to me about professional matters. Eddie said, "Pat would like you to read this paper. He says he'd value your opinion." I read it, told Eddie what I thought, and he told Pat.

Eddie gets angry at anyone who criticizes me. This is unfortunate at a conference table. I have a quaint notion, too, that he does not like to be criticized in my presence. Chivalry has handicapped me a little—it has made it easy for me to stay away from the sound of fury.

In spite of these drawbacks I am a matchmaker, and would like to see married couples go to work together. It is a satisfying fusion when it works out well.

Psychologists tell us there is a strong drive of the two sexes to return to the original bisexual organism from which they derived. It is nice to think that Eddie and I are merging into one being, as the marriage ceremony puts it, in a symbolic-spiritual sense.

People used to ask, "Do you really work with your husband?" and, with a look of faint horror, withdraw to the other side of the room. There has been a slight change. Twice within the last month young women have asked me, "Is it easy to work with your husband? Tell me, is it hard? What difficulties do I have to watch for? Would you advise me to do it?"

It seems to me that double partnership doubles everything, especially the pleasanter aspects—respect, loyalty, admiration, affection.

You have so many interests in common that you can't possibly be bored with one another. You have something to talk about day and night. You are never silent at meals. I wonder what couples talk about who share only half their interests.

It must be very lonely for husbands and wives who have large areas of isolated activity and live in separate compartments. He might want to tell her what the market did today to his sales chart, but he obeys the old tyrannous adage, "Don't bring your business home with you."

Eddie would burst if he couldn't talk about his profession at home. And I would feel lonesome if I didn't know what occupied most of his attention.

Eddie said, "Why should a man try to divide himself into two parts, think about one set of ideas until five o'clock and refuse to think about them at six o'clock? If his work bores him at night he ought to find another occupation. And if his wife isn't interested in his work he oughtn't to have married her."

If you work with your husband you can admire him as much as you like without any feelings of guilt, a pleasure that is denied women who work with other men. I praised Eddie one evening and Lyman Bryson said, "Now you're talking like a partner, not a wife."

Geoffrey Hellman invited me to talk about Eddie. "Now tell me some bad things about him." I gaped. Eddie, like all husbands, is perfect and if he had any faults I would not have revealed them.

On my seventeenth birthday Eddie arranged a surprise party. He led me to a large bonfire on the beach surrounded by twenty-five boys and girls shrieking, "Happy Birthday." You watch this same organizing skill grow until you are convinced there is no problem in public relations too difficult for him to solve. You know, too, that he has courage enough to say, "This can't be done," or to say, "This can be done," when everybody else thinks otherwise.

You watch the speed and intensity of his work. While another person might wonder whether to start something today or next week, Eddie picks up the telephone and does the job. He dictates a chapter of his book (and complains, "I can't seem to do more than 5,000 words a day on this thing"), then rushed to a meeting of the Multiple Sclerosis Society, comes back to analyze a foreign country in terms of an American company's policy and product, telephones at length to clients, advises a corporation to consider guaranteed employment, and on and on without pause in the flow, but with constant interruption of one task by another. I coax him home and postpone dinner, hoping he will rest before eating.

Eddie was responsible for many firsts of which I am reasonably proud. He invented the name public relations counsel; he laid the groundwork for the profession in practice and presented theory in books and in university courses.

We both realized in the early 1920's that public relations was potentially a powerful machine that could conceivably help civilization or wreck democracy, depending on who used it for what ends.

Public relations could become a sloganizing machine, a news-mongering device, an instrument for narcissists and exhibitionists. It could become plain silly or it could become a Frankenstein, as it did in Germany and Russia. It could also become a fine tool for education.

That is why we believe that because public relations is a function in the public interest, and that its practitioners should be licensed to practice on the basis of education, training and character, just as doctors, lawyers and accountants are.

Women who see only one side of their husbands' life miss surprising switches in personality. At home Eddie always bowed meekly to the children's demands, and this was delightful because I knew he was anything but meek in his work. Living and working with a person of extraordinary energy can be exhausting, but you understand this strange current that doesn't stop day or night. You try to engage all of his triple attention at home. He wants to hear about your grand-niece (aged three) and her jealousy of her sister (aged one) while he hurls himself to a couch to read the paper, listen to a WQXR news broadcast, and at the same time cut through a problem that has bothered you for weeks.

Occasionally you feel he is lighting a stove with dynamite. And you wonder if that is because he is a man. And are most men like that? You go to the office next morning, and there he is, phoning, reading his mail and dictating a research procedure.

Of course I know why double partnership is wonderful for me. Eddie seems to think it is wonderful for him, but he will have to explain why himself.

As far as I am concerned, double partnership has made it possible for me to do the jobs that I am expected to do as a woman without conflicting with his idea of my professional duties.

Women have always worked at home for love, and because men like it that way, we shall continue for a while to conform to this ancient pattern. Although I am an amateur in our home, I am a professional in our office; but the change takes place automatically without any change in my personality or modification of our attitude toward each other. Unplanned and almost instinctive, the metamorphosis is a direct response to a culture syndrome.

"Aren't you coming to the office with me?" Eddie asked shortly after we were married. I looked around our lovely studio in Washington Mews. He, too, looked at the flowering plants and the cut flowers that seemed so essential and appropriate to our honeymoon state of mind. "I think I'd better stay home and fix the flowers, don't you?" He agreed and a new precedent in attendance was established that held for minor emergencies of decorating, plumbing and house painting. By the time our first child appeared the relative values of professional and personal obligations had been quietly and satisfactorily established.

Pregnancy is a labor concept in the personnel department of many a big business. It calls into consideration such bristling factors as absenteeism, turnover, waste of in-training effort, sickness benefit, act of God, equal pay for equal work, child welfare plans and other things.

When your husband is your partner he will cooperate with you all the way from whims to letting you work as long as you want to. He makes it possible for you to act as you feel, that pregnancy is a healthy, normal function of life.

He is equally cooperative after your babies arrive. He loves them, too, and wants them well cared for. You will have no difficulty in getting him to keep your job open if you stay home when they are ill, when they are too cute to leave, when the nurse is out, when you want to take them to the park for the sheer pleasure of it, when you investigate schools, when you go to school to see what is going on. He may grumble that you are neglecting him and your other job. But he leaves you in no doubt that he approves your maternal duties and pleasures.

This is one of the disadvantages in double partnership;

your husband places a higher value on your professional work than on your work at home. Although he knows what you can do in the office he is convinced that you are willfully inefficient if you spend half a day planning your daughter's engagement reception.

"For heaven's sake, it will take care of itself." He wants you to sit in his office and listen to him dictate a memorandum on stock-holder relations.

Eddie liked the idea of sharing his professional life with his family so much that he even tried to make his little daughters his partners. Little Dorie was permitted to see an advance model of a Kelvinator refrigerator under conditions of the utmost secrecy. Later she was taken to a home economics convention in Pittsburgh where she asked each expert, "Are you married? Why not?" She believed their answers were also classified.

Annie, at the age of seven or thereabouts, visiting Mr. Deupree, then President of Procter & Gamble, confided to him, engagingly, "I like Lux much better than Camay, don't you?" At this point Eddie's desire to mix business and parental love subsided.

Women who have jobs away from their husbands often have special difficulties. The old stale theme of home versus career never seems to die down. It was news in 1914 as the subject of many interviews for the *Tribune*. It was still highly controversial news in the twenties when Eddie and I were press agents for "The Famous Mrs. Fair." It is a poignant problem today to all the husbands who want total devotion from their wife. ("My God, she spends hours on the phone discussing the damnedest problems of her students.") It is a bitter problem to women who realize late in life that they have willingly done what they had to, not what they wanted to. ("Look at me sitting here in Palm Beach in January. I go to the Caribbean, to the Riviera, to Norway. What kind of a life is that? I'm eighty-four. Do you know what I want to do? I want to have my own little jewelry store. But my sons won't let me. 'You worked hard enough all your life,' they say, and they take me to the station again.")

Differences in earning power can be explosive. "There is no use lying to your husband about the size of your pay check, because income taxes tell all," said a decorator who earns a good deal more than her husband, a chemist. A successful gynecologist's husband is a stock broker. He got fighting mad when she was called out on night cases. By the time she got back from helping a new baby into the world, "He was roaring drunk." So she decided on separate bedrooms and telephones. "Now he doesn't know when I'm called out and everything is fine." Percy White and his wife Polly Arnold headed competitive market research organizations. They underbid each other for clients, kept trade secrets from each other but met amicably at their Connecticut hearth. Eddie advised them to merge, and assured them that their personal relations would be enhanced by commercial union. After years of split interests, they relaxed in the warmth of mutual problems and triumphs.

The clock is a tyrant to women with separate careers. Her job won't give her time off for household and maternal essentials, like teething and mothers' meetings at school. And at the other end she finds an impatient husband. "The other evening I was fifteen minutes late coming home and there he was at the corner waving his arms at the policeman," said a harassed young woman lawyer with the ambition to become a judge.

Obviously not every man can share jobs with his wife. For one thing, it would upset union wage scales that might be financially tipped in favor of males. A coal miner would be unpopular if he brought his wife along from portal to portal.

Certainly a steel puddler can't have his wife working at the next puddle.

The wife of a philosopher is not necessarily a scholar. She may be a landscape gardener. In spite of this, wives often are expected to be experts in their husbands' special fields, as if the skills were contagious. And most wives throughout history have been unofficial aides to their husbands. This used to be called indirect influence.

I listened to a playwright answer telephone calls from her husband's patients. "Is the pain very bad? The doctor will be over in an hour." "Does he have fever? When the doctor calls up I'll tell him about it. No, I wouldn't do a thing if I were you." She dialed for her husband. "I think Mrs. K. needs you in a hurry."

I know several painters' wives who act as managers, carrying pictures to galleries and talking with editors. A commentator relies on his wife for clipping out-of-the-way items that his staff of researchers can't seem to find. A traveling salesman gets fat envelopes from his wife, filled with photographs of their two babies, gossip and news that she has clipped from his trade journals. Another young wife of a business beginner is studying stenography. She told me, "He works so hard and late the least I can do is to help him write up his reports and type his letters."

Any woman who works outside the home and keeps house is in danger of developing a double sense of guilt. She probably overworks in both jobs to placate her conscience. Whether she works with her husband or with someone else, she has to prove to herself that she is not shirking office work for household duties, and she works overtime at housewifery because she spends her days at an office.

We feel guilty because we are expected to do so many things for which we haven't time, training or skill.

I don't work harder than most women. Less, by measure

of the ancient proverb, "Some respit to husbands the weather may send, But huswiue's affaires haue neuer an end." The problem is still valid, especially for double-duty women, whether they scrub office floors, keep house for other women, turn lathes in factories or count blood cells in laboratories. They are all career women as surely as the executive behind an office desk or the judge in a city court. For all of these women official hours of work are added to the expected hours of work as mother and housewife.

Everyone knows women like the one who supports a sick husband and a son by working as housekeeper for other people from nine to five six days a week, and often as waitress until eleven or twelve at night. She does her own housework besides and is the comforting wife and mother whom her husband and son depend on. She is sweet and uncomplaining.

Mrs. O'Rourke, my mother's seamstress, was a widow with six little children. She took in waistlines, lowered and raised skirts, broadened and narrowed shoulders, took her youngest to school, cooked, cleaned, washed laundry and dishes, mended for them, nursed them when they got sick, wept during a three-days' wake when the six-year-old was slaughtered by an automobile while she was delivering clothes to her customers.

One of my neighbors, a farmer's wife, cared for her house and her family of eight, raised chickens, cultivated a large kitchen garden, ran church sociables, and looked like a pictrue from *Vogue* when her husband came in for supper.

I am lucky in being able to do the work I like in pleasant company, rather than having to spend my days at unfriendly work among uncongenial surroundings. If I had had to work only at housekeeping I would probably have adjusted, as millions of women do.

Eddie, however, likes only my office job, and tries to protect me from the rigors of work in the home.

"Why don't you rest?" he asks in exasperation. "The people won't come for dinner for half an hour."

"I just want to see if the cook . . ."

"No," he interrupts violently, "I won't have you do housework. I'll go down and tell her."

CHAPTER TEN

Butterfly in Armor

A psychologically complete and sincere autobiography would contain so many indiscretions about family, friends and foes, many of whom are living, that in my case as with everyone else, it ought flatly to be ruled out. What makes all autobiographies worthless is their essential mendacity.

Sigmund Freud
From a letter to Edward L. Bernays
October 8, 1929

It is very strange. My whole life has been devoted wholeheartedly to love, and I still know nothing about it. I am not sure that there is any essential difference between the emotion that goes out to one's family, to an abstraction of truth or justice, to something beautiful, or to the shrill shrieks of anonymous children playing in the street.

Love is not only affection for parents or children, for one's husband, or the dynamics of sex. A feeling for Bach's *B Minor Mass* or the twilight view of Florence from Fiesole, for my mother and father when I was a child, for Dorie's lilting giggle and serious frown, for Annie's dimple and her *avant-garde* voice, are the same in quality, if not in intensity. I love the ocean anywhere, kindness and moral courage. I love a beautiful turn of words, S. Hayakawa's evocative logic, Mozart's everlastingly unequaled letters, his *Piano Concerto in D Minor,* the other-worldliness of Bartok's *Bluebeard's Castle,* and the first faint yellow mist of spring on the backyard trees. I love anything my daughters do or say, and any way they look, smudged or englamored.

All these have filled my life almost to the exclusion of everything peripheral else. And yet, although they are all part of the same thing, I know nothing about the whole or its parts.

It is commonly supposed, of course, that love is a woman's whole life. It is also generally agreed that with men it is a thing apart. But this I cannot believe. Men need, want and think about love as much as women do. For every Elizabeth Barrett Browning, there have been hundreds of John Donnes.

Therefore I am amazed at my courage in writing about a subject that has been so well thought over by so many billions of men and women. However, because this little book discusses the many functions of any normal woman, I must put down something above love in my life. What do I know about it?

I read Ovid's *Art of Love* when I was a student at college, but I doubt that I profited much from it. Fraser's *Golden Bough* taught me a good deal about things other than love. Havelock Ellis was embarrassing. A few anthropologists seemed to run intellectual peep-shows. Sociologists today talk about "affectional relationships." Kinsey's next book perhaps will tell us why "Fifty Million Perverts Can't Be Wrong." I have never looked at how-to-books on the mechanics of sex because I am puritanical. I have been married to one man for thirty-three years, an uneventful history that in individuals, as in nations, makes for happiness. I know nothing, but feel everything about Love. Everybody goes on talking, writing and singing about love. Everybody in the world seems to have written a poem, sent a valentine, composed a serenade or fought a duel about love. The placid lions in front of the New York Public Library are doubtless ruminating about the 1,572 books listed under Love in the card catalogue files upstairs.

In spite of this we know more about the atmosphere on Venus than we know about the feelings of one human being for another. We can predict to the milli-fraction of a second when man-assembled elements will meet for destruction. There is no predictability about the effect of one person on another. The world is deficient in this most beneficent of all powers, in spite of the inspired efforts of religions, philosophies and intuitive individuals.

Freud was right. We learn to love at home, within the family. Unless our libido gets an early start, it will probably not reach its goal of mature love. My own preoccupation with the good will and affection of my parents dominated my childhood, and of my brilliant, fascinating brother Leon who was two years older in July and August, and three years older from September to my next birthday. My little sister Bea was much too young for me to love her, and cherubic Ira was practically not born yet.

I adored Grandpa and my uncle who promised to marry me. He was a handsome old man of twenty-five. I fell in love with my cousin Leo, who lived in Albany and spent most summers with us on Long Island. He, too, promised to marry me. My uncle's best friend, Charlie Spitz (Mr. Saliva, of course) took me to the opera when I was ten years old, and that night I fell in love with Caruso.

My first accessible love was Leon's best friend, Ned Wendt, whose nose humped fascinatingly in the middle and tipped up at the end. He was excessively sophisticated and he was eighteen, five years older than I. I was stupefied with awe the first time I met him. Leon, he and I walked up Fifth Avenue.

"Why don't you say something?" Leon hissed. But I couldn't think of anything worth saying. I thought of pointing out a shop window, but realized in time that he might think I was hinting.

Most of my childhood loves were unattainable, as if my spiritual muscles had to be developed safely in a laboratory. All through our teens boys and girls suffered from frustrated love. We consoled one another constantly. I suppose we were careful not to fall in love with an attainable object until we were ready for marriage. But we were not conscious of such drives. That is the appeal of the Frank Sinatras, the Eddie Fishers and other television loves today.

I worshipped Governor Teddy Roosevelt when I was ten. Joan Sperling and I made up plays, taking turns at the role of Teddy and Heroine. He dashed up a hill on horseback to rescue Joan or me. I knew that someday I would marry him. His own large family was quite irrelevant. I loved David Mannes, the violinist. After a concert of the New York Symphony Society I telephoned him merely for the ineffable joy of hearing his voice.

"Will you give my little son violin lessons?" I asked. My best friend, Minnie Frank, stood next to me at the wall phone in the hall and whispered, "Make your voice deeper."

My notions about love came from romantic literature—*Paul and Virginia, The Crisis, Monsieur Beaucaire, The Gentleman from Indiana,* and not from an understanding of the emotions of my parents, whose obvious love for each other was tedious and slightly incongruous in such aged people. Passion was Donald Brian making grease-paint love in *The Merry Widow* and had no relationship to my parents' silly habit of holding hands as they walked down the street.

We knew the word gender but never heard of sex.

No Provençal troubadour of the eleventh century was as romantic as we were in our early adolescence. Amy Weil loved Ned Wendt too and all her friends held their breath as they passed his home, in tribute to her (probabaly unrecognized by him) devotion. My friends reported to me any slight news about Sandy whom I loved desperately although he didn't know me at all. His face was David Warfield superimposed on Abraham Lincoln, and his lips and hands fluttered adorably as he ran around the tennis court.

Our language had a faint resemblance to Goethe's and

Lessing's *Sturm und Drang* period, to Racine, who tore the stars from the heavens to prove his passion. Verbally, all that we knew—people, events, food, scenery and everything else—were awful, cute, adorable, thrilling, wonderful and marvelous. The pet words of today's adolescents are more restrained and probably more cynical. People are drips, schmoos, grease balls. Things are sharp or keen when they are pleasant. Events are cool when they are overwhelmingly good.

We spent much of our time on vague insubstantial love. We scarcely knew the difference between reality and fantasy affection.

Love was the main interest of our adolescence. Love was the glittering, prickly thread that wound in and around the tough rope by which we pulled ourselves from infancy to adult bewilderment. No one is really adult until that thread is smooth. Love was agonized waiting for a telephone call, a letter; it was yearning for a smile, a walk in the park; a glimpse of Aucassin. Love was magic. It was extrasensory perception.

We were taught nothing about love or sex. Nobody helped us through the pangs of disillusionment, or the excitement of mutuality, as they call it today.

Occasionally I thought, won't it be wonderful when I'm old and won't have to love any more? Perhaps I was not altogether wrong. Nothing is more painful than the fruitless pangs of adolescent stumblings toward the goal of a procreative union. Perhaps I would have matured more easily if I had been advised or helped through this difficult period of trial. Unfortunately, our parents had not today's understanding, negligible as it is, of that mystic function, adolescence. My adolescence lasted until someone admired my gray hair on my fiftieth birthday.

My outlook was subject to a succession of violent thrills, ecstasies and despairs. I sobbed through Beethoven's *Eroica*

Symphony. Shooting a basket from center was totally enchanting; so was writing my first imaginative composition at school (I think it was called "Soliloquy of a Grandfather's Clock"), dancing to *The Blue Danube* with the best dancer in the world, or anyway, the best dancer I knew, reading Browning for the first and tenth time, reading innumerable romances that distorted life completely and compellingly, and listening again and again to Caruso's round golden voice.

All this kept pace with love for the little boy whose voice was changing, for the middle-sized boy with football hair who was a hero on the gridiron but was too bashful to talk to you, for the mature and sophisticated high-school senior who read Baudelaire in the original, for the six-foot-two, pidgeon-toed athlete at Yale who despised books but revered college spirit, for the boy who was as beautiful as an Arrow-collar man and who was snatched from you by your best friend (her perfidy as great as her immorality, you decided, when you learned that she let him kiss her) and for other boys until you were out of the adolescent category and no longer subject for this little memoir on old-fashioned mate selection.

I loved a golden-haired boy madly because he was quite beautiful and all my friends were jealous. We buried noble resolves in the sand under an orange harvest moon. I adored a tall, dark man because he had a fascinating split in his lip. I used to dramatize myself into the kind of giddy, irrational girl I thought he might love. This love was divine until one day I forgot my role and talked seriously about a new book. He left me forever.

When I think of the boys I might have married if they had proposed to me—a moron, a genius, an athlete, an esthete and a soul-torn introvert! Luckily they were still in school or fresh out of college. I was sure of only one thing and that was that I would marry an athlete. (Eddie thinks fresh air is unwholesome, and the sun is poisonous.)

My brother was so fickle and apparently charming that I was immensely popular with girls who haunted our house, hoping for a glimpse of him. Elsa, with enormous blue eyes and golden braids, used to show me her diary. Each day's pages, starting, "Darling, dearest Diary," had a margin of red crayon hearts named Leon. Minnie, Grace and Edie and a dozen others told me about their love for him, and what he had said. I decided to write a book, *Confessions of a Sister*.

Beatrice, my young sister, was a notable heartbreaker. Gil, who looked like Lincoln and wrote fine poetry; Jacques, tall and handsome, who seemed to spend his life avoiding school at fashionable resorts in the South of France; a preacher's son whom she mothered; a newspaper man who terrified her almost into an elopement; a sweet shy law student who died in the battle of the Argonne Forest.

We had to learn how to talk to boys, how to behave toward boys, how to be little girls and then young ladies. Every new boy was practice material in the process of learning. Sex knowledge waited on the other side of the wedding ring.

We accepted without question all sorts of unreasonable ground rules. No one had to explain taboos or general principles of conduct to us. They were as inevitable as the clothes that covered us, layer on layer. We knew that girls must never take the initiative, or be obviously receptive.

"Can I come over tonight?"

"Well, let me see. Yes, I think it would be all right," was bold encouragement.

"Will you write me at college?"

"If you write first, I will." He must not know that you like him, that you wait painfully for the telephone to ring.

You had to pretend you were ignorant and stupid, and at the same time you had to be bright and entertaining. No matter how you hated small talk, that was what you used for communication until you had mastered the art of listening to him. If he was boring, you learned to smile, open your eyes wide and shut your ears tight. If you had any ideas you had to slip them in through the conversational back door.

It was possible, however, to discuss a few burning issues—Omar Khayyam, Platonic Love, Sincerity, Dutch Treat. One boy let me pay for a cup of coffee to show his sincerity.

When we were about seventeen years old, Eddie introduced me to an entire new vocabulary of ideas. As we swam at Deal Beach, he told us about psychophysical parallelism, the chemistry of sex attraction and Freudian concepts of repression and the subconscious. Elsa, beyond her depth, sank for an instant and came up sputtering and giggling, "Mr. Fundamentals."

Psychological chatter gradually altered our speech and thoughts and freed us from the tyranny of pretending to be idiots. We found that boys no longer despised us for talking sensibly about trial marriage, free love, world peace or poetry. Sitting on the grass under a tree, Melville Herskovits, unaware how he was flattering me, talked about primitive tribes and skull measurements.

Whether we spent hours sailing on the Sound, singing around the piano or discussing eternal verities on the porch, we were pure and decorous. There was not a wolf in a sleigh ride. We were completely chaste. It was fast to hold hands, unless you were telling fortunes, which we frequently did. No good-night kiss at the door, no smooching, no necking, no petting. I became engaged to a boy because I suddenly wanted him to kiss me.

"Will you be my bride?" he asked.

"Yes," I said, and found myself in a man's arms.

My daughter, at about the same age, asked me, "Mommy, did I have to let him kiss me good night? I didn't want to."

When I was sixteen, I wanted to find out what handholding was like. To be safe, I chose a dull boy for the experiment. The result was negative. His hand was merely a wad of dry flesh. Naïve? Yes. But our astute teenagers today are not too much wiser.

My daughter's classmate made a very distant but parallel observation. "Girls are dopes to sleep with a boy they love. I'd never do that. But I might sleep with someone I didn't love. I probably would. No hesitation about that."

Feebly, I suggested, "Perhaps that might distort your ideas about sex."

My mother's problems seem to have been simple, but possibly weren't more bearable than mine or my children's. She managed to become affianced to two men and jilt them before she found Pop. She was nearly jilted by Pop because he thought her dress too immodest for a lady.

"My new dress, for New Year's Day," she explained. "It was beautiful, gray silk and steel passementerie, long sleeves and high in back. But just cut down the least bit in front. To here," she pointed to the hollow spot at the base of her neck. "He was furious and said he would never come back." Moth smiled. "But he came back that evening."

I can remember Dorie and Annie trying on new dresses and asking, "Are you sure it's sexy?"

Today's children and young women have more violent problems. Do boys lose respect for girls who neck? Can a girl be popular if she doesn't neck? Do men respect girls who are not virgins? Do girls have to lose their virginity to get along with boys at all? Will the boy she loves want his wife to be a virgin?

Sex never stops bedeviling the young. We suffered vague, unexpressed longings, half-perceived discontents and deliberate blindness in my repressed, inhibited youth. Yet today's youngsters have a more difficult apprenticeship to love. They are pioneers, they must make their own rules and policies, and decide on their own course of action. Their problems, even though they are discussable, are as painful as those of my generation.

"He looks at me so, ugh, it's simply horrible," said my fifteen-year-old daughter. "I can't bear it."

"But you loved him passionately last week. You wanted him to love you," I pointed out.

"Yes, I know," she wailed, "but I didn't know he would look so awful when he did. Won't I ever love a man who loves me? Why do all the drips fall in love with me? Why do I always have to love someone who doesn't love me?"

The adolescent experimentation that we hear so much about today is only partly biological. It may be a response to some personality need; a girl has to prove to herself that she is popular, or she may reach out blindly, sometimes compulsively, for love and security. Mainly, however, this quest for experience and knowledge is cultural. A girl has to go along with the customs of her group in every country and every age.

The present generation of teen-agers has the special responsibilities and difficulties of self-determination. They are permitted to stay out at night until they are too tired or too bored to do anything but go home. They can drink, and many of them do. A group of fifteen-year-old girls at my house some years ago talked about drinking.

"Well, she went to his birthday party anyway, after all she said about him. There was a bottle of champagne at everyone's place at dinner. Well, she woke up the next morning in her own room, all dressed on her own bed, and she doesn't know how she got there."

Mother, on Saturday nights, used to go to the Mt. Nebo Lodge, the Fidelio Club, Mt. Sinai Lodge and Terrace Garden. Grandpa, wearing white tie and tails, was her escort. He drank wine or beer and Mother had soft drinks and danced with family friends.

I was not allowed to drink anything stronger than lemonade in public, but my own best friend, a spirited and lovely girl, went to a road-house with a man alone. I was loyal. Nevertheless the wash of scandal separated us.

Today a girl must be thoroughly efficient in sin in order to cause talk. Dorie at Radcliffe telephoned me, "Mommy, do you object if I study in Al's room at night?" I answered, "Certainly not, if it doesn't start a scandal." "It won't," she assured me. It is customary for girls to visit boys now, whether the boys have their own apartments, or still decorate their parents' home.

Usually a chaperone was a guarantee of virtue. Chaperones. What a cumbersome, bumbling institution! By all the laws of Freud we should have developed neuroses. We should have rebelled and gone to the dogs; or, frustrated, we should have developed monumental inhibitions or aggressions. I could go to the theatre in the afternoon, take daylight walks in the country and sit in the parlor with a boy until eleven o'clock at night. Five minutes after that deadline my father's voice rang down the stairs, "Doris, don't you think it's time for your young man to go home?" This humiliating and irrational custom assumed that virtue could be enforced by surveillance. Why did parents believe that vice slept all day and bounded from its cave at sundown?

Innocently I shocked my father so severely that he crossed the thin line between being a man of very few words and being speechless. Aunt Blanche had arranged for me to visit her nephew, who was laid up with an eye ailment. The room was dim, and as we talked, we could hear the murmur of his mother's voice conversing with our aunt. It was definitely romantic. He was beautiful, I loved him, and I was a missionary serving humanity in a bold and daring way.

"You visited a man in his *bedroom*?" asked Pop when I returned home.

"He was sick," I protested, "and Aunt Blanche and his mother were there." Pop's eyes looked hurt and bewildered. His daughter was amoral.

Even at the age of twenty-one I was not allowed to go to the theatre alone with a man, and whether or not we were chaperoned, the play had to be chosen most carefully. My father never learned that when Rhoda's mother took Rhoda, Walter, Arthur and me to the theatre just before graduation from Barnard College, the play we saw was Brieux's *Damaged Goods.* The tickets were provided by Eddie, who was producer, with Richard Bennett, of this sensational play about syphilis. Walter and Arthur, strained and worried, occasionally rolled their eyes at each other. They shouldn't have been at that play with nice girls.

We went to dances and were protected from mischance by dance cards and by escorts who made sure that the cards were completed filled. We went to well-chaperoned week-end parties, for skating in New Jersey, for tobogganing in Pittsfield and canoeing in the Adirondacks. Although we hated our parents' watchfulness, we felt on the whole that we were a pretty emancipated generation. We were not, we said proudly, *jeunes filles de bonne famille.*

I wonder now what our parents had to worry about. They knew where we were, what we were doing and with whom. It must have been placid and safe to be the parent of daughters. Sons were turned over to their fathers for sex guidance, if the fathers weren't too bashful.

I asked four women eating lunch in our backyard what sort of success they had in trying to advise their children about sex.

"We all try to help them but it's no good. They won't listen to us," said the successful author of a soap-opera serial.

"They know too much, and they think we know too little," complained a textile designer.

"It's true. We're too muddled ourselves about biology and sex to be any good to them. Did you ever read Sorokin's book, *The Ways and Power of Love?* He's head of that

Research Center in Creative Altruism at Harvard. Even the experts are muddled." This from a slangy musicologist.

"Maybe the experts are muddled. But we're too cocksure about what is good and bad about sex. No wonder my children won't listen to us."

Occasionally my friends' children ask my advice. I always have a fine glow of morality when I tell them that chastity is good business for young women, and at the same time I always have an icy fear that I may be wrong—that I may be talking from the past, not from the present or from any conceivable future. Perhaps the socio-cultural biological aim of our present society may be changing completely. Not long ago the eighteen-year-old daughter of a friend announced to me:

"I'm going to have an affair with —— (a famous playwright)." Of course she wanted me to dissuade her. I told her that sex relations in our present society have a greater psychological effect on women than on men. I gave her biological data that seemed to surprise her.

"I guess you're right. It was a silly idea. I'll wait. But for goodness' sake, don't tell my mother. She'd die."

Her mother had said a few days before, "My daughter tells me everything. We are absolutely frank with each other." There is candor up to a point between generations.

I enjoyed trying to keep open the channels of communication between my children and me. Sometimes the results were surprising.

"What are you reading?" asked Anne, at an age when I had known nothing about sex except the facts of procreation. Anne looked over my shoulder at a report of Professor George Murdock's ideas about pre-marital sexual experimentation.

"Hm," she commented, "he seems to think we have no proof that pre-marital chastity has any scientific value. Well, I don't agree with him," she said decidedly.

"Why?"

"I don't mean morally. I just think it isn't safe for a girl anyway. And if you think it through, the world would be so full of illegitimate children that there wouldn't be such a thing as a family."

"What about contraceptives?" I asked her.

"They're not sure. Everybody knows there are accidents. Anyway, I guess I'm old-fashioned. I think that sort of thing should be saved for marriage," said my daughter.

I wanted to know more. "What about the necessity Dr. Murdock talks about, to find relief from sexual frustration?"

Anne dismissed him carelessly, as she hitched her saddle bag over her shoulder. "The sex act isn't that important. People put too much stress on it. Good-bye, Mommy, I've got to go." She turned around at the door and waved. "Remember your daughter is chaste."

Sowing wild oats is considered essential today. But it may not be good social agriculture.

Occasionally I suspect young people are not as wise as their words. Their semantics is way ahead of their knowledge. My daughters' four high-school friends, a Princeton senior and two Marines were discussing life. The Marines presumably had had some little experience, but I stopped wool-gathering about something one of them had said a few sentences back, just in time to hear Jim announce blandly, "Of course, sex dies out after three years of marriage." They agreed that was a reasonable assumption.

Nothing conversational is taboo, from biology to frustration. They know all about emotional responses, rejection, substitution, identification, transvestism, inversions, perversions, and other matters sacred, profane, normal and abnormal that I had never heard of when I was twenty.

The presidents of two first-rank colleges, discussing such things one evening, seemed not to be disturbed by sexual precocity.

"I doubt if more than twenty per cent of girls are virgins by senior year," said the president of one college.

"You're way off," said the other president. "I'd give it ten per cent at the most."

"I don't believe it," I said, purely emotionally.

Two high-school teachers were surprisingly nostalgic about their youthful moments of decision.

The somewhat pompous history teacher said, "I'll regret all my life that I put sex to the test before I was married. I'll always have a sense of guilt." She reached for a pretzel. "Besides, I might have married him. You know, an inexperienced girl thinks she has to marry a man if she sleeps with him."

"I don't agree at all," interrupted the math teacher. She looked quite stern, although she is happily married to her second husband. "I regret that I didn't put sex to the test—you put that so nicely—before my first marriage. My life would have been better. It's the only civilized thing to do."

"Would you," I asked, hating to be personal, "would you want your daughter to?"

"Of course."

I know something about the loves and lives of primitive tribes and sophisticated and bucolic civilizations, but it didn't help me much in making sense of this muddled adult picture.

Mate selection is quite a gamble in our society, with scarcely any rules to guide young players. Most of my relatives are contentedly married—Bea and Martin, Ira and Eleanor, Dorie and Dick and Anne and Justin.

I am amazed that my own marriage is still good and new after thirty-three years. Eddie and I were lucky to have picked each other. We both had fallen in love with wrong people so often that I cannot believe either instinct or wisdom had anything to do with it.

Family-relations experts have improvised a few do's and don'ts, many of them based on old biases and new preconceived notions, on fantasy, superstition and accidental propinquity. We let clichés guide us. "Love is blind." (Why try to think things out?) "Opposites attract." (It doesn't matter a bit that you have no interests in common.) "Love at first sight." (This is the rationale for loving or not loving anybody, for marrying or not marrying him.) "Birds of a feather." (Choose a mate whose background is like yours. Sometimes tribalism or clannishness.)

It is wonderful, even miraculous that any two people can pull happiness from the jackstraw heap of personalities waiting to be married. And yet the majority of marriages even in this restless era find some measure of happiness and two-thirds maintain continuity.

Even as children we made firm decisions about the kind of man we were to marry. Alice, Constance and I stopped skating for a minute in Central Park to consider this subject. "I'm going to marry a rich man," said Connie, and she eventually did. Alice said, "I am going to marry a poor man," and, like the majority of people in this world, she did. I didn't care if he was rich or poor. I wanted only love. But if he had to be anything, he would be an athlete. Eddie walks reluctantly from home on Sixty-third Street to our office on Sixty-fourth Street and back again. I used to be a good athlete, but I should hate to live on the run now.

I was frightened by a fortune teller's prediction that I would receive nine proposals of marriage before my husband took over. I didn't know boys made as many errors in the game of mate selection as girls did. A young bond salesman thought we were meant for each other because I allowed him to talk to me about bonds—the only subject he was interested in. A delightful preacher asked, "Could you ever marry a minister?" Not realizing he meant it until someone later told me he had been serious, I answered in general, "Good heavens, no." An intense young doctor thought he loved me. And I thought perhaps I loved him, until he drove into a street too soon in delivering me home. He slapped his forehead and groaned. Perhaps wisely, we abandoned each other because of an act we both thought was a symbolic rejection.

My daughters, aware of the id, the ego and the new supraconscious, would say about one of their friends who is an old maid of twenty-five, "She can accept passion, but she can't give love. That's why she has to be psychoanalyzed." Shakespeare and today's psychiatry-oriented young men and women all agree that love is a malady that ends in a bust-up, or lasts forever.

Fortunately I was married before the flapper age, because that was a period of mate betrayal rather than mate selection. It was a disgusting time of sexy antics, promiscuous public lovemaking and drunkenness. In spite of F. Scott Fitzgerald, devotee and prophet of disorder, there was little that was pretty about the conduct of people of all ages who caricatured and burlesqued adolescence. Stockings rolled below the knees, naked thighs, corsets checked in country-club cloakrooms, condoms in the family car in the morning, somersaults and handstands by underclad girls in the drawing room, wife-stealing, husband-snatching, change partners, parties that lasted four days, white tie and tails on the avenue in midmorning, aspirin jags, opium smokes in Paris. (What is the funny smell in this room? Oh, we had a party last night.) Walls hung in black velvet, carpet and couch in black velvet and table covered in black velvet, orange cushions and orange chinaware. A friend who would not permit her husband to take the dog walking because the dog knew where she went on illicit visits in Paris.

All these things were quick, bawdy and cynical substitutes for mate selection. I could not have competed. For that matter, I believe that only a small percentage of young people were active members of the flapper age. Most of us were normal, well behaved and well enough adjusted not to have to explode into social rebellion.

Historians, anthropologists, clergymen, marriage-brokers,

soothsayers and parents, all have tried their hand at the job of finding the right parents for the children of the future. They have sold brides, bought grooms, for land, cows, jewels, money, titles, status, dowries and settlements. Love has been considered all important—and negligible. Parents have done everything, and they have completely washed their hands of the whole business. Whatever methods we have tried so far have left us with too many discontented husbands and wives and too many children on whom such discontent has rebounded.

My parents had a slightly negative approach toward our suitors. Pop simply permitted us to go with a boy, or forbade it. "He is not a suitable companion for you." When Bea was sixteen she fell in love with an older man, a novelist. Pop forbade her to see him, because his eyes never quite looked into other people's eyes. In the light of his subsequent history, I believe that his truly shifty eyes indicated a sense of guilt because he had a black streak of sadism. Pop was right for the wrong reason. At any rate, she has had a long, happy marriage with Martin who has only desirable characteristics.

Pop had a chilling contempt for most of my friends, except Eddie, who was inevitable. I believe they did not mind Pop's forbidding manner too much, because that was the attitude of so many fathers.

Eddie's parents were so delighted when he married me that I would have suspected, if I hadn't known it, that he had conspicuous social initiative and mobility. For a wedding present, Eddie's father gave me a large package with a letter, dated five years previously, saying, "For Doris, when she shall have married Edward." He smiled somewhat grimly and said, "This has been in the vault all this time."

If you are thoughtful, you wonder why you as a parent today, after thousands of civilized years' attention to family welfare, are powerless to help your children make good marriages. Nevertheless, most parents start thinking about being helpful in fantasy even before the child is born, continue through mud-pie days, early birthday parties and summers in the country. Their active planning grows less as the child grows older and really needs more help, from cokes to cocktails, from Freshman English to the G.I. Bill, from going steady to the trembling march to the altar.

"Oh, you're the mother of Doris," said a handsomely dressed woman when we were introduced at a dinner party. She blushed pleasantly and explained, "Did you know that my Jackie is terribly in love with her?" Doris and Jackie were freshmen in play school in the four-year-old group.

A few years later during a parents' meeting at the Brearley School, a mother who is quite successful in her own social life whispered to me, "How do you find boys for your daughters? Jane doesn't know any at all."

Somewhat later, at a welfare board meeting, a harried woman asked, "Do you think I could arrange to have your daughter meet my son? He's been away at school and college for eight years, and doesn't know a single girl in New York." We arranged it in a thoroughly roundabout way, so that neither side would suspect interference with their independence.

While parents today are aware of the need to help their children, they are also aware that there is not much they can do. They try, but fairly hopelessly, to apply the wisdom of the ages, knowing that there is very little wisdom in mate hunting.

Eddie and I used to worry each other all night long about Anne's latest unsuitable suitor. We usually felt she was on the edge of a marital precipice and we must yank her back to safety. What luck that she and Justin found each other.

Here is the great debate among parents. After dinner not long ago, interruptions grew fierce.

"You must try to stop a bad love affair."

"Bobby is in love with a terrible girl. I use every catty, underhanded trick I can think up to break it off. I gouge and I scratch."

"It won't work," said a small tender woman, just recovered from a nervous breakdown. "I forbade Alice to see Grove. You know what happened. They eloped. Only eighteen." She shook her head.

"Of course it won't work," said a psychiatrist. "Opposition increases the attachment. They marry sometimes just to prove their independence from their parents."

"But why?" I asked, bewildered. "You tell your children what medicine to take for a sore throat. Why should you stop advising them when they need help most? Why should parents assume a non-directive attitude about marriage?"

"Have you ever interfered?" someone asked the psychiatrist.

She grinned and said, "Our sixteen-year-old daughter was in love with a thoroughly unfortunate young man. He was, we thought, quite neurotic, with apparent anti-social potentialities."

"What did you do?"

"Against my own advice, I tried to make her see him as he was." She paused. "Then my husband took over and interviewed him. Voices in the library grew louder and louder. Then there was the clatter of feet on the stairs and my husband's voice shouting, 'Get out! Go away! Don't come back!' "

"What happened then?"

"He continued to come back, and she got to hate us very much. Then one day she came running in, quite breathless and excited.

" 'I don't love him a bit. What on earth did I ever see in

that awful, conceited, vain little man? Why didn't you tell me what he was like?'

"What made you dislike him so suddenly?

" 'He took me to Tiffany's to choose an engagement ring. I looked at them and got sick to my stomach. He wasn't the man I wanted to marry. I ran home.' "

The ineptness of parents and the increase in divorce have led our teen-agers to take charge of their own pre-courtship. While it is true that the majority of marriages in this country remain legally binding, it is also true that separation, desertion and rejection leave so many children below the line of love that they fear broken homes more than they fear the atom bomb. A little girl told me, "There is nothing more terrible than divorce. The one thing we all hope and pray for is that we won't be divorced."

Here I think is the reason for that comparatively new and revolutionary phenomenon, 'going steady.' It combines the virtues of an orderly pre-courtship procedure and an attempt to learn how to be faithful. It is miniature monogamy.

When Dorie was sixteen years old, she asked me solemnly, "Mommy, do you mind if Frankie and I go steady?" I answered glibly, I am afraid, "Of course I don't mind as long as you see other boys too." Her bewildered look showed me that I didn't know what going steady meant. For a while I watched this new device—everybody dropped from her life but this one cute boy. What happened, I wondered, in small communities where there is so little social mobility anyway that no one meets anybody outside his own circle? What chance has friendship to grow naturally in a large city where social mobility is so great? She went to parties, it is true, but wherever she and Frank went, they stuck together like castaways on a raft. They might just as well have put on their party clothes, turned on the radio and danced together at home. It seemed, however, that getting to know one another might be a helpful prelude to the mature relationship of marriage. It might be, I thought, a brave and wise approach to the whole problem.

To help me understand this new custom, I made a wide survey among high-school principals, sociologists, psychologists and psychiatrists, hoping that they would solve this riddle of practical young idealists. Whenever a new problem has come up in my job as wife, housekeeper and mother, I have found it helpful to read a few books, spend a few days in special libraries, talk to authorities, or make a fairly broad survey. I found that experts were, for the large part, completely bewildered about going steady. Pedagogues, sociologists and others whose minds are somewhat institutional in orientation were on the whole against this revolutionary change. Psychiatrists who like people better than institutions and who like to push down tottering walls were in favor of going steady. Dr. Frederic Wertham, for instance, who has fought valiantly against comics, said to me, "I am for fidelity even in adolescents."

Hundreds of youngsters all over the country, whether they were over-serious, intellectual, lyrical or flippant, had great desire for security and stability through love in this irate century. Some of the most telling conversations were gathered for me by Richard Adler, then a bright and sensitive young man to whom adolescents talked easily and freely.

I was psychologically and emotionally illiterate when I married. I had learned little of value from the varied and non-intimate relationships that had disturbed my adolescence. Today's adolescents are more intelligent, they are braver and they are wiser. They are determined to make better lives for themselves. And they have broadened out their emotions to include the world outside themselves, a world they hope to improve.

Will ambivalence, that emotional state in which hate lies

like a worm in the heart of love, remain a classic symptom or will it have a classic cure? At a convention dinner given for wives of company men, I listened, surprised, while the talk for four hours was concentrated on their much loved mother and father. Eighteen middle-aged women told how unreasonable, how demanding, possessive, egocentric and devoted their parents were.

"She is a remarkable old lady. But what she makes me go through!"

"If I don't spend a full hour with her every day, she raises the dickens with me. And all I have to do with five school children."

"Papa won't call me up. Oh, no, but if I don't invite him for dinner on Sunday he gets gout, and his neighbor . . ."

Parents of young children sometimes believe that love between generations is as easy as rolling off a log in a spring freshet. Unfortunately, both children and parents are unprepared for cooling-off periods. Child-parent love at some point must change into friendship-love or it becomes a burden; frustrated, it has a way of turning negative.

"Mommy, what do you think? My friends like you." This was the surprised comment of a newly-married lad.

"Why shouldn't they?" his mother asked rashly.

He was embarrassed and apologetic. "They all loathe their parents. They think parents are the lowest thing on earth." When I heard this, I seemed to remember vaguely that children half a century ago hated to have their mothers come to school. It was proper to try not to see them.

I have seen thinly veiled contempt in the eyes of some adult children for their parents, and I have listened to some parents talk unpleasantly about their married children. I know many Cornelias whose jewels have lost their luster.

Perhaps these parents have lost some of their ability to love, have encysted their affections, have retained only disappointment, criticism and bitterness. "Think of the dreadful girl he married. She writes his letters to me. The impertinence. I don't even read them."

Such extremes fortunately are rare. But there is enough universal truth in them to explain the popularity of *Life with Father.* (Father wasn't really as cranky, and Mother wasn't as tricky as I used to think.) It is true, however, that parent-child love normally and naturally alters in character. But no one knows in what direction or to what extent.

On Ed Murrow's program J. Robert Oppenheimer talked of an undefined factor in physics that cannot be measured in space or in time, but is related to both. There was a startling undertone implicit in this calmly stated idea. Perhaps there is a factor in love, too, that has not yet been defined in terms of any relationship.

Love, by signs, symbols, but not by definition, lights a lady's cigarette and walks a dog on a sleety midnight. Love chases a hat skittering across traffic lanes, and love gives your shirt to a friend. Love carries the bride over the threshold and wheels babies in the park. Love cooks dinner and comforts a tired husband. Love shrinks oceans and paints a harbor for remembrance.

I was lucky to have married Eddie, because affection spreads out limitlessly. More than a quarter of a century later our two daughters fortunately married men with whom they will find lifelong happiness.

Yet there is not enough love to keep the world at peace. There is not enough to keep neighbors at peace, or members of Congress, or colleagues in business or religious groups armed against one another. The Golden Rule is still in the pot of gold at the rainbow's end. Nearly all religions give love the highest value, the Bible, the Bhagavad-Gita, the Dhammapada; scriptures of Christianity, of Taoism, Confucianism, Hinduism, Judaism, Mohammedanism and others.

I know only that love is not easy, unless you have a talent for it, and are willing to work at it. Love must be learned young, if it is to function effectively. This world will survive if people can learn to love one another. And the impetus must come from an informed and benign nursery.

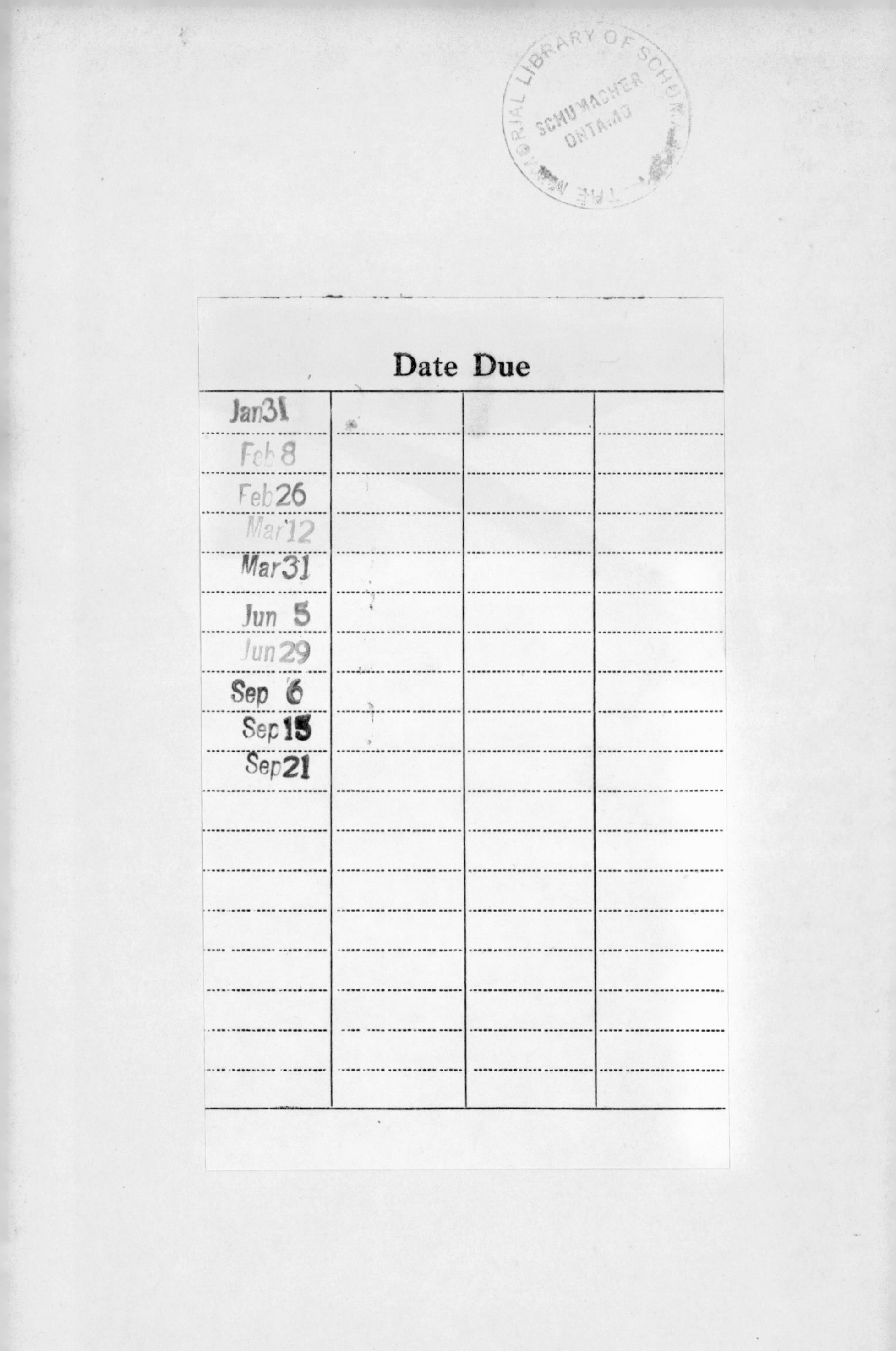
THE MEMORIAL LIBRARY OF SCHUMACHER
SCHUMACHER
ONTARIO
Date Due
Jan31
Feb 8
Feb26
Mar12
Mar31
Jun 5
Jun29
Sep 6
Sep15
Sep21